T0268168

DOGFIGHT 8

MiG-21 "Fishbed"

Opposing *Rolling Thunder* 1966–68

István Toperczer

OSPREY PUBLISHING
Bloomsbury Publishing Plc
Kemp House, Chawley Park, Cumnor Hill, Oxford,
OX2 9PH, UK
29 Earlsfort Terrace, Dublin 2, Ireland
1385 Broadway, 5th Floor, New York, NY 10018, USA
E-mail; info@ospreypublishing.com
www.ospreypublishing.com

OSPREY is a trademark of Osprey Publishing Ltd

First published in Great Britain in 2023

© Osprey Publishing Ltd, 2023

All rights reserved. No part of this publication may be reproduced or transmitted in any form or by any means, electronic or mechanical, including photocopying, recording, or any information storage or retrieval system, without prior permission in writing from the publishers.

A catalog record for this book is available from the British Library.

ISBN: PB: 9781472857569; eBook: 9781472857590; ePDF: 9781472857583; XML: 9781472857576

23 24 25 26 27 10 9 8 7 6 5 4 3 2 1

Edited by Tony Holmes
Cover and battlescene artwork by Gareth Hector
Ribbon and tactical diagrams by Tim Brown
Armament artworks by Jim Laurier
Maps by www.bounford.com
Index by Zoe Ross
Typeset by PDQ Digital Media Solutions, UK
Printed and bound in India by Replika Press Private Ltd.

Osprey Publishing supports the Woodland Trust, the UK's leading woodland conservation charity.

To find out more about our authors and books visit www.ospreypublishing.com. Here you will find extracts, author interviews, details of forthcoming events and the option to sign up for our newsletter.

Front Cover Artwork: On the morning of November 18, 1967, 16 F-105s and their F-4 fighter escorts targeted SAM sites and AAA positions in advance of a larger formation of Thunderchiefs bound for Hanoi and Noi Bai air base. Amongst the VPAF 921st FR pilots scrambled to intercept the approaching jets were future ace Pham Thanh Ngan and Nguyen Van Coc, who were masters at employing the "fast attack–deep penetration" tactic favored by veteran MiG-21 pilots.

Scrambled at 0748 hrs, the pair flew out over Thanh Son in their MiG-21PFLs "Red 4324"and "Red 4326." Ten minutes later, Coc spotted enemy aircraft flying from Yen Chau to Ha Hoa at a distance of eight kilometers. He and Ngan rapidly climbed to gain an altitude advantage of 1,500–2,000m over the USAF jets before attacking them. Ngan fired an R-3S missile that hit *Wild Weasel* F-105F 63-8295 flown by Maj O. M. Dardeau and Capt E. W. Lehnhoff of the 34th TFS/388th TFW. The Thunderchief burst into flames and crashed in Van Du hamlet, along the banks of the Lo River.

After launching his first missile, Ngan saw another F-105 and fired his second missile at it, but he had to break off his pursuit seconds later. Although Ngan had not witnessed his R-3S hit its target, Coc, flying as his wingman, saw the F-105 damaged by the exploding missile. Coc then chased down a third Thunderchief and fired a single R-3S. The weapon hit Lt Col W. N. Reed's F-105D 60-0497 of the 469th TFS/388th TFW, the aircraft also bursting into flames, as seen in this artwork. The two MiG-21s pilots then made good their escape. (Cover artwork by Gareth Hector)

Previous Page: A groundcrewman congratulates the pilot of MiG-21PFL "Red 4320" "Fishbed-D" at Noi Bai following a successful mission. The first batch of MiG-21PFLs reached North Vietnam in December 1965, and following their assembly they were were declared combat-ready by March 1966. The "L" designation in PFL stood for "Locator," indicating that this variant was fitted with a different sensor suite to the standard MiG-21PF. PFLs were also locally referred to as "PFVs," with the "V" denoting their service in Vietnam. (István Toperczer Collection)

Acknowledgments – The Author would like to extend his thanks to the following individuals for their valued assistance over the years: Nguyen Van Coc, Vu Ngoc Dinh, Nguyen Van Nghia, Ha Quang Hung, Lu Thong (deceased), Nguyen Sy Hung, Nguyen Nam Lien, Bui Van Co, Nguyen Huu Dac, Nguyen Xuan At (deceased), Tran Dinh Kiem, Nguyen Van Dinh, Phan Truong Son, Phan Le Lam Son, Nguyen Manh Hung, Le Nguyen Bao, Sándor Doma, Zoltán Földvári, Gergely Gróf, István Hérincs, Sándor Kontsagh, Zoltán Lente, Róbert Lévai, Frank Olynyk (deceased), Zoltán Pintér, László Reindl, Róbert Sándor Simon, Raphaël Didierjean Vincent, RepTár Museum of Szolnok, the Ministry of Defence of Vietnam, the Embassy of the Socialist Republic of Vietnam in Budapest, the Embassy of the Hungarian Republic in Hanoi and the various military museums of Vietnam.

Dedication – This book is dedicated to the memory of VPAF combat photographer Nguyen Xuat At.

Contents

CHAPTER 1 **IN BATTLE** • **4**

CHAPTER 2 **SETTING THE SCENE** • **9**

CHAPTER 3 **PATH TO COMBAT** • **22**

CHAPTER 4 **WEAPON OF WAR** • **27**

CHAPTER 5 **ART OF WAR** • **43**

CHAPTER 6 **COMBAT** • **56**

SELECTED SOURCES • **79**

INDEX • **80**

CHAPTER 1
IN BATTLE

After a number of large-scale USAF attacks in the Hanoi area had failed to achieve the desired results during April 1967, the HQ of the Vietnam People's Air Force (VPAF) predicted that the fighter-bombers would again attempt to strike targets southwest of Hanoi on the last day of the month. Sure enough, on the 30th, radio communication between 20 F-105 Thunderchiefs and eight escorting F-4 Phantom IIs was detected as the aircraft approached the Yen Phu electrical power plant in Hanoi.

Leading the Thunderchiefs was the *Iron Hand* flight (call-sign "Carbine") of the 357th Tactical Fighter Squadron (TFS), part of the 355th Tactical Fighter Wing (TFW). Consisting of three *Wild Weasel* F-105Fs and a single F-105D, it was responsible for tackling any surface to air missile (SAM) sites that might threaten the main strike force.

The 921st Fighter Regiment (FR) commander Tran Manh and deputy regiment commander Tran Hanh were in the command duty post that day, while the duty ground control officer was Pham Minh Cay. Regiment pilots, and future aces, Nguyen Ngoc Do and Nguyen Van Coc had been instructed to man their MiG-21PFLs ("Red 4227" and "Red 4325") at the "on duty" location at Noi Bai, northwest of Hanoi. After receiving the aircraft from the technical team, Do discussed with his wingman the tactics they would use if the enemy was engaged:

> Listen Coc, when we meet the enemy, there will be multiple flights. We will try to get in behind the lead flight, and I'll attack first. You keep your distance and observe my attack, and make sure to fly at a higher altitude than me. You must keep a close eye on both my maneuvers and those of the enemy.

Nguyen Ngoc Do was flying MiG-21PFL "Red 4227" on April 30 when he and his wingman, Nguyen Van Coc, fired R-3Ss from both aircraft to down two Thunderchiefs of the 357th TFS's *Iron Hand* flight targeting SAM sites ahead of a 355th TFW strike on the Yen Phu electrical power plant in Hanoi. (István Toperczer Collection)

> When I reach the optimum range to attack, I'll call you over the radio. I will also call you when I fire a missile. It's your job to spot if the missile hits its target. After firing, I'll break off to the right and pull up, at which point you need to choose a target and attack. I'll then turn back into the enemy formation to observe you, telling you the optimum moment when to fire your missile. If the distance is too great for the weapon I will tell you so, and you can alter your approach. Once you are at an effective range I'll order you to fire. I need you to be very calm, not hasty. What do you think?

Coc replied, "I totally agree with your plan. Ready to follow your command, flight leader!"

At 1459 hrs, shortly after radio communication between the enemy jets had been detected, Manh contacted VPAF Command and requested permission to scramble the 921st FR's "on duty" MiG-21s. Do, in "Red 4227," and Coc, in "Red 4325," were duly ordered to take off and head for an area south of Moc Chau. Once there, the pair were instructed to orbit at an altitude of 3,500m over Thanh Son–Phu Tho. At 1516 hrs VPAF radar detected target aircraft heading north towards Yen Chau. Approximately four minutes later, the MiG pilots visually acquired the enemy jets below them and 30 degrees off to the left. After spotting their targets, they switched on their afterburners and dived in the direction the five F-105 flights, which were flying in "column formation."

Do radioed Coc, "Do you see them? Four are flying beside the cloud. No fighters behind!" Do then contacted his Ground Control Intercept (GCI) controller, requesting permission to attack. He was quickly given approval, Coc recalling:

> Do ordered me to "Drop your external fuel tank, begin to attack, turn with me!" and he quickly followed the enemy flights, which were still unaware of our

OPPOSITE
On April 30, 1967, future VPAF ace Nguyen Ngoc Do claimed the first of his victories when he shot down F-105F 62-4447 of the 357th TFS/355th TFW during an engagement over Vinh Phu Province. Maj L. K. Thorsness and Capt H. E. Johnson successfully ejected and became PoWs. Do is seen here in late November 1967, by which time his flying jacket had been adorned with five "Huy Hieu Bac Ho" ("Uncle Ho") badges. Each one had been awarded to him for downing an enemy aircraft. (István Toperczer Collection)

presence. "I'll follow the last one. No. 2 [Coc], you pay attention to the one ahead. Distance is five kilometers now. Continue to approach! Distance is 3,000m. Too far, do not fire! Distance is 2,000m. Good aiming. I'll fire now."

I watched the missile leave his aircraft. He had aimed at the F-105 flying ahead. Tracing a green line through the sky, the weapon flew straight into the enemy aircraft, which was immediately engulfed in flames. Unable to contain my joy, I shouted, "He's burning! You hit him, Flight Leader!" The GCI controller was not happy with my outburst, and I was told, "Attention, calm down!" Do then also radioed, "No. 2, calm down!"

Do had shot down F-105F 62-4447 (call-sign "Carbine 3"), flown by Maj L. K. Thorsness and Electronic Warfare Officer Capt H. E. Johnson from the 357th TFS, and both men successfully ejected from their jet and were eventually captured. Following the downing of "Carbine 3," Do broke off right from the remaining aircraft in "Carbine" flight, before quickly turning back in their direction in order to cover Coc's attack. Having checked his wingman's position behind the Thunderchiefs, he radioed Coc:

It's okay, your aim is good but you are still too far away for a missile shot. Continue to approach. Distance is 3,000m now, hold your fire! Good range now, steady your jet.

Coc checked the parameters for the missile shot and confirmed what his Flight Leader had just told him. Do then gave him one final instruction – "Good range. Fire!" Coc had fully exploited the momentary confusion that had gripped "Carbine" flight following the demise of "Carbine 3," increasing his speed and getting onto the tail of "Carbine 4" – F-105D 59-1726 flown by 1Lt R. A. Abbott of the 354th TFS/355th TFW. Keeping his jet as stable as possible, Coc centered the Thunderchief in his optical gunsight and pressed the missile launch button at a range of 2,000m and a speed of 1,200km/h. Seconds after being fired, the R-3S hit the F-105D and virtually broke the USAF fighter-bomber in half. The shattered aircraft burst into flames and crashed into the ground near Thanh Son, Abbott having ejected shortly after his jet was struck.

Do shouted, "Bravo, you hit it!" and then ordered Coc to "Break off right!" Do, who was flying to the right of his wingman, also broke away to allow Coc to perform the evasive maneuver. The two jets then quickly reformed, with Do rocking his wings to congratulate Coc on his first aerial success – he would claim nine more before the end of the conflict. Their

The second Thunderchief to fall to the 921st FR on April 30 was claimed by future ranking VPAF ace Nguyen Van Coc. F-105D 59-1726, flown by 1Lt R. A. Abbott, was the first of nine aircraft (five of which were Thunderchiefs) credited to Coc during *Rolling Thunder*. In this photograph, taken later in the war, he is wearing a ZSh-3M helmet whilst sat in a MiG-21PFM at Noi Bai. (István Toperczer Collection)

GCI controller then told them to break off the engagement and return to base, Coc following Do back to Noi Bai.

The wreckage of one of the downed F-105s from the 355th TFW smoulders in a rice paddy field near Phu Tho shortly after the aircraft was shot down on April 30. All four crewmen that ejected from the Thunderchiefs were captured. (István Toperczer Collection)

Lessons Learned

After no fewer than nine MiG-21s were claimed by F-4Cs from the 8th TFW between January 2–6, 1967, the VPAF had temporarily suspended combat operations for the 921st FR so that its pilots could regroup following these chastening losses. The unit was ready to return to action by late April 1967, and the victories achieved on the 30th came as a nasty shock to the USAF – it had never lost multiple aircraft to MiG-21s before.

The aerial engagements fought on the last day of April had seen the 921st use pairs of MiG-21s to strike at the center of the F-105 formations for the very first time, and the results the VPAF pilots achieved proved the effectiveness of this tactic. The combination of high speed, visual target acquisition (confirmed by ground-based radar) and the correct missile engagement range had surprised "Carbine" flight. The 921st had spent four months perfecting the "hit-and-run" tactic used on April 30, with every pilot being drilled on precisely when to turn on their radar and fire their missile. The performance of Do and Coc validated the work done by the regiment since its poor showing in January, boosting the morale of the 921st and restoring confidence in the MiG-21's combat abilities.

The loss of two F-105s in quick succession had been relayed by surviving Thunderchief pilots to "Red Crown" (the call-sign for the fighter controller embarked in a radar-equipped US Navy warship offshore in the Gulf of Tonkin), which in turn scrambled search and rescue (SAR) aircraft to look for the downed crews. 355th TFW vice-commander Col J. M. Broughton, who was leading the strike, immediately aborted the mission and concentrated on supporting the rescue attempt. Two minutes behind "Carbine" flight, Broughton told Maj E. Dobson, leading "Tomahawk" flight, to fly RESCAP (Rescue Combat Air Patrol) over the downed airmen until the SAR force arrived. "Tomahawk" flight duly split so that two aircraft were orbiting low over the downed airmen and two were higher up acting as radio relays to "Red Crown" and the approaching SAR A-1 Skyraider "Sandy" aircraft. Meanwhile, the remaining F-105s set off to find tankers to refuel so that they could return and take over RESCAP duties if required.

VPAF Command decided that the orbiting RESCAP F-105s were prime targets for attack, and at 1629 hrs the 921st FR scrambled two more MiG-21PFLs flown by Le Trong Huyen and Vu Ngoc Dinh. Forty-five minutes later, just as Maj A. J. Lenski (call-sign "Tomahawk 3") and Capt J. S. Abbott (call-sign "Tomahawk 4") were about to turn south and head for a tanker after running low on fuel, they were attacked from behind by Huyen and Dinh.

At 1715 hrs, whilst on a heading of approximately 260 degrees, Lenski "felt a jolt and heard a thud" and immediately called Abbott to break left "because of MiGs." As Lenski broke left and down, he saw a MiG-21 off to the right at "three o'clock high." This was the "Fishbed" flown by Dinh, who completed a left banking turn turn across the top of "Tomahawk 3" after firing his "Atoll" at the lead F-105. Lenski then spotted Huyen's MiG-21 as it engaged Abbott's Thunderchief, warning "Tomahawk 4" that he was in imminent danger. Both pilots lit their afterburners and accelerated to Mach 0.95, jinking in an attempt to throw off their pursuers as they headed for cloud cover at an altitude of 3,650m. Lenski asked Abbott several times if he "had him [the MiG] in sight," and "Tomahawk 4" answered affirmatively. At 1720 hrs, approximately ten seconds after his last radio transmission, Lenski looked behind him and saw a fireball, which he assumed was Abbott's aircraft.

Again, the 921st pilots had used "hit-and-run" tactics to telling effect, much to the surprise of their opponents. In less than a minute Huyen and Dinh had each hit an F-105D with an "Atoll" missile. They then pulled up into a climb, broke off the engagement and returned to Noi Bai. Abbott's F-105D (61-0130 of the 333rd TFS/355th TFW) caught fire and he was forced to eject into captivity. Lenski's Thunderchief was badly damaged, although he managed to escape into cloud and only just made it to a tanker before running out of fuel. He then limped back to Udorn, in Thailand. The SAR effort for the four downed airmen failed due to a combination of heavy, and accurate, anti-aircraft artillery (AAA) fire and mechanical problems.

Six distinct piles of wreckage can be clearly seen in this elevated view of a downed aircraft "graveyard" somewhere in North Vietnam. (István Toperczer Collection)

CHAPTER 2
SETTING THE SCENE

Operation *Rolling Thunder* was a gradual and sustained aerial campaign conducted by the Pacific Air Force's 2nd Air Division (replaced by the Seventh Air Force on April 1, 1966), the US Navy's Task Force (TF) 77 and the Republic of Vietnam Air Force (RVNAF) against North Vietnam from March 2, 1965 until November 2, 1968. At its peak, *Rolling Thunder* was the most intensive aerial battle of the Cold War. Its primary purpose was to destroy the transportation system, industrial base, and air defenses of North Vietnam, stop the influx of soldiers and weaponry into South Vietnam, persuade North Vietnam to stop supporting the communist uprising in South Vietnam, and boost the sagging morale of the Saigon regime.

Achieving these goals was hampered by the restrictions imposed on the US government by its allies and the military aid and assistance that North Vietnam received from the Soviet Union, the People's Republic of China, and North Korea. The weaponry supplied to the VPAF in particular allowed it to establish one of the most sophisticated air defense systems, comprising SAMs, AAA, and MiG fighters (MiG-17s, MiG-19s, and MiG-21s), ever fielded against US military aircraft.

Rolling Thunder missions commenced on March 2, 1965 when USAF F-100D Super Sabres and F-105D Thunderchiefs and RVNAF A-1H Skyraiders struck targets at Quang Khe naval base and an ammunition depot at Xom Bang, with modest success. Carrier-based A-1 Skyraiders, A-4 Skyhawks, and F-8 Crusaders participated in the first *Rolling Thunder* mission by carrier-based aircraft on March 15 when US Navy, USAF, and RVNAF units struck an ammunition depot southwest of Phu Quy. USAF aircraft bombed Dong Hoi airfield in the first such attack on a VPAF base at the end of March.

Air operations over North Vietnam during *Rolling Thunder* were conducted by the USAF and the US Navy in alternate three-hour intervals. Should strikes be delayed through weather or technical malfunctions, chaos often ensued over the target area. Furthermore, in the early months of the campaign there was little in the way of operational coordination between individual units, and it

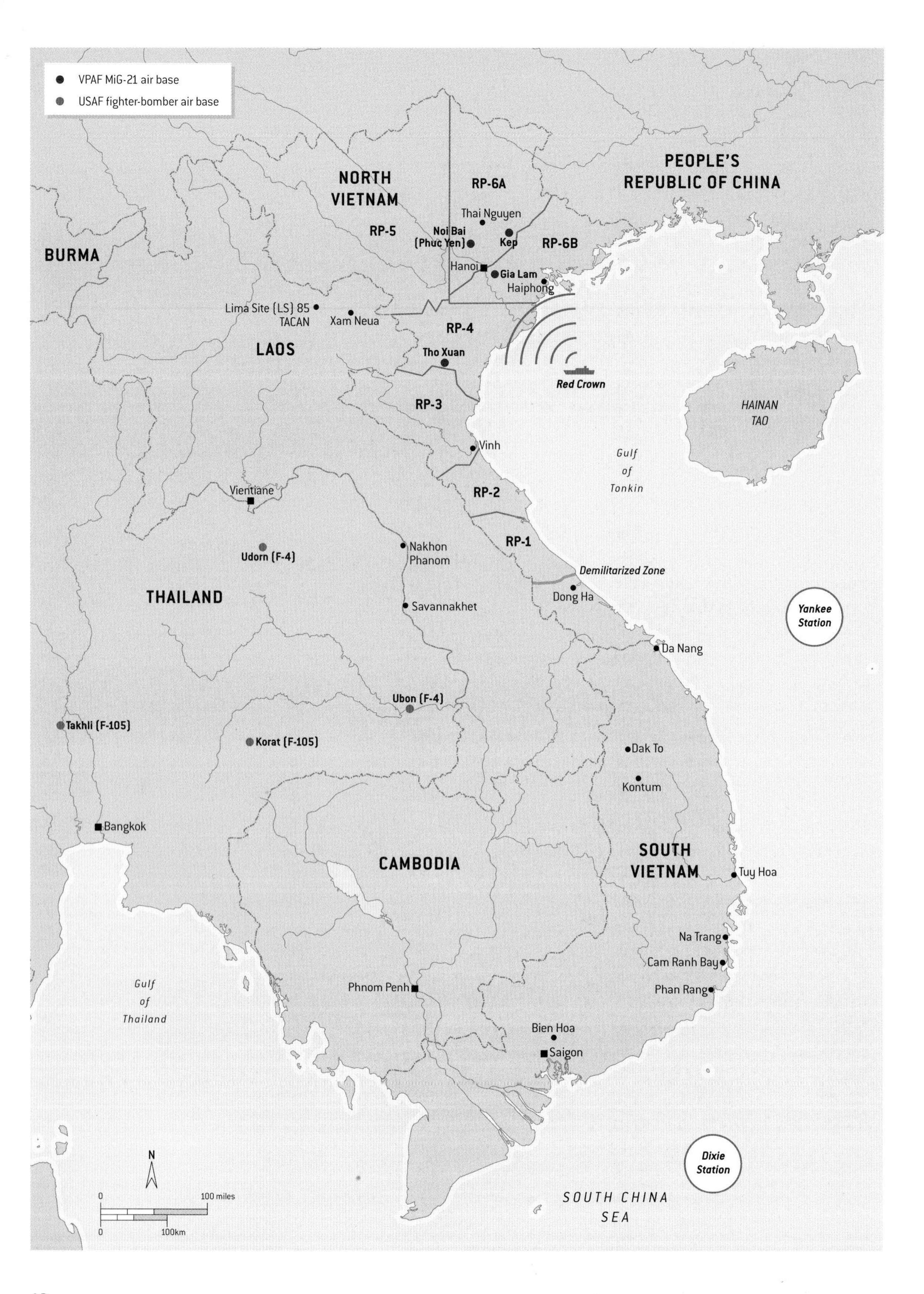
VPAF MiG-21 air base
USAF fighter-bomber air base
PEOPLE'S REPUBLIC OF CHINA
NORTH VIETNAM
RP-6A
Thai Nguyen
RP-5
Noi Bai (Phuc Yen)
Kep
RP-6B
BURMA
Hanoi
Gia Lam
Haiphong
Lima Site (LS) 85 TACAN
Xam Neua
RP-4
LAOS
Tho Xuan
Red Crown
HAINAN TAO
RP-3
Vinh
Gulf of Tonkin
Vientiane
RP-2
RP-1
Udorn (F-4)
Nakhon Phanom
Demilitarized Zone
THAILAND
Dong Ha
Savannakhet
Yankee Station
Da Nang
Ubon (F-4)
Takhli (F-105)
Korat (F-105)
Dak To
Kontum
Bangkok
SOUTH VIETNAM
CAMBODIA
Tuy Hoa
Na Trang
Cam Ranh Bay
Gulf of Thailand
Phnom Penh
Phan Rang
Bien Hoa
Saigon
Dixie Station
N
0
100 miles
0
100km
SOUTH CHINA SEA

was not unheard of for aircraft from two different carrier air wings to attack targets in the same area without prior knowledge of each other's mission.

In an effort to eradicate such operational inefficiencies, a USAF–US Navy coordinating team divided North Vietnam into six sectors in December 1965. The sectors were christened "Route Packages" (routinely abbreviated to "RPs") and were designated 1 to 6. Initially, the USAF and the US Navy operated in all Route Packages at assigned times, alternating "RPs" every six weeks. In April 1966, Adm U. S. Grant Sharp, Jr., Commander-in-Chief, US Pacific Command, added a seventh area by dividing RP-6 into two sectors – 6A to the north and west of Hanoi and 6B to the south and east of the city, the sectors being divided by the main railway line to China.

TF 77 handled operations in RP-2, RP-3, RP-4, and RP-6B, as they were all bordered to the east by the Gulf of Tonkin, whilst the USAF was given RP-1, RP-5, and RP-6A. RP-1 was on the border with South Vietnam, while the two sectors of RP-6 were considered the best defended and most dangerous airspace in the world at that time as they included both Hanoi and Haiphong and the vast majority of the strategic targets in North Vietnam.

On April 3–4, 1965, the VPAF sent its MiG-17 "Frescos" into action against American aircraft over North Vietnam for the very first time, resulting in an F-8 Crusader being badly damaged and two F-105s shot down. The USAF quickly realized that its bomb-laden Thunderchiefs could not defend themselves against the highly agile and heavily armed MiG-17s, so F-4 Phantom IIs were tasked with protecting them. Although the "Fresco" remained a threat to all American aircraft, if the latter attempted to maneuver with the VPAF jet at slower speeds and lower altitudes, the MiG-17 found the missile-armed Phantom II a deadlier opponent than the F-105.

Senior officers in the VPAF had recognized the threat posed by the F-4 prior to the start of *Rolling Thunder*, and following persistent lobbying by the North Vietnamese Ministry of Defence (MoD), the Soviet Union agreed in February 1965 to the supply of two strategic anti-aircraft weapons in the form of the S-75 Dvina/Volhov (SA-2 "Guideline") SAM and the MiG-21 "Fishbed." In preparation for the arrival of the latter, the MoD sent flying cadets and groundcrew to the Soviet Union for training in April 1965.

A number of pilots from the MiG-17-equipped 921st FR were also chosen for conversion training onto the MiG-21 based on their performance in the "Fresco," the regiment switching to the "Fishbed" once the first examples reached North Vietnam in late 1965. The 921st would be equipped with all three MiG-21 variants (F-13, PFL, and PFM) fielded by the VPAF in opposition to *Rolling Thunder*.

The fighters soon to see combat with the North Vietnamese could trace their lineage back to the late 1950s. When the Mikoyan-Gurevich Ye-6 (essentially a pre-production MiG-21) began its flight test program on May 20, 1958, the aircraft was the culmination of a series of five development types that commenced with the Ye-2 in February 1955. The program aimed to produce a supersonic land-based single-seat point-defense day fighter to protect Soviet military installations from high-flying bombers. Lacking sophisticated radars and missiles, the MiGs of this era relied upon speed to pursue their targets, firing short-range missiles or heavy-caliber cannon when in range.

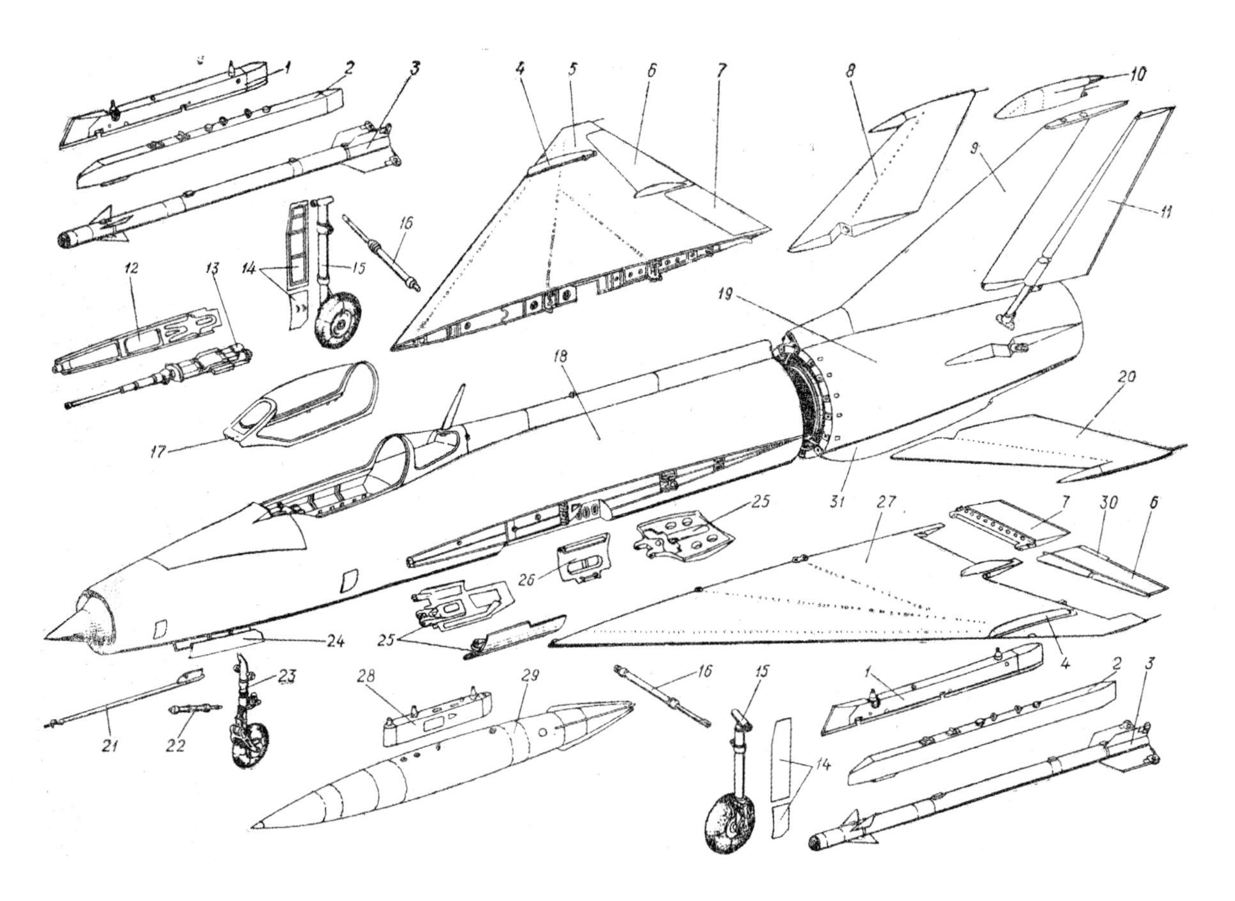

This MiG-21F-13 diagram was included in the Soviet servicing manual supplied with the aircraft to air forces that flew the aircraft. Amongst the parts that are numbered are the wing pylons (1) for the APU-13 rail launchers (2) to which the K-13 (R-3S) AAMs were attached missiles (3); the internally mounted NR-30 cannon (13); and 490-liter PTB-490 centerline fuel tank (29). (István Toperczer Collection)

The MiG-21's role demanded a lightweight short-range single-seater that was capable of reaching a target at supersonic speed and destroying it with minimal gun or missile armament.

Although influenced by the experiences of MiG-15 pilots in the Korean War, the MiG-21 had primarily been designed in response to a Soviet air force (*Voyenno-vozdushnye sily* – VVS) requirement for a faster fighter capable of taking on the USAF's F-100 Super Sabre interceptor and B-47 Stratojet and B-52 Stratofortress bombers. The advent of the supersonic B-58 Hustler bomber added Mach 2 speed at 65,000ft to the list of potential threat aircraft that it needed to oppose. Rapid rate of climb and high maneuverability were paramount, but night or all-weather capability was not required. Like other contemporary VVS fighters, the new contender had to be simple in construction and undemanding on maintenance.

In the spring of 1953, the MiG OKB (experimental aircraft design bureau) was instructed to produce a lightweight, supersonic interceptor, while the rival Sukhoi OKB proceeded with heavier, radar-equipped, all-weather fighters. Several very different MiG prototypes were built following the wind-tunnel testing of models that tried out a range of possible configurations in the air. The first, designated the Ye-2, had sharply swept wings and a tail unit like the MiG-19.

The other configuration, flight-tested as the Ye-4, used a delta (or, in Russian, "balalaika") wing attached to a Ye-2 fuselage. This flew on June 16, 1955, and quickly began to resemble the definitive MiG-21. Using a delta eased the application of the recently established "area rule" concept, which, by reducing "wave drag" over the fuselage, made supersonic flight more feasible. Unlike most contemporary Western delta-wing designs such as the Vulcan, Mirage III, and F-102 Delta Dagger, the MiG gave its first delta a sharply-swept, all-moving horizontal tail. In comparative trials, the Ye-4 wing demonstrated slightly higher speed, better rate of roll, and a larger fuel capacity than the swept-wing Ye-2.

Great fighter designs rely on outstanding engine technology, and the team headed by S. K. Tumansky, which had produced the afterburning RD-9 engine for the MiG-19, created the R-11. Despite being the same size as the RD-9, it yielded 50 per cent more thrust. The powerplant was installed in the Ye-5 – a modified Ye-4 with a new airbrake and three large fences above each wing to improve stability. The nose was lengthened, a bigger afterburner was installed, and the engine proved successful, despite early fires and turbine failures.

Final prototypes, designated Ye-6s, were followed by ten pre-production MiG-21s built at the state-owned Tbilisi plant. These had uprated RD-11F-300 engines, squared-off wingtips, and two underwing hardpoints. Tail surfaces were enlarged, a single ventral fin replaced two smaller strakes, and the air intake, with its three-position conical center-body, was modified to improve airflow at high angles of attack. The front-hinged cockpit canopy was strengthened, although not enough to save test pilot Vladimir Nefyedov when the Ye-6 prototype crashed inverted after an engine flameout.

A side-view and cutaway drawing of the MiG-21F-13, also sourced from the Mikoyan-Gurevich manual for the aircraft. Amongst the parts identified are the nose cone (10) housing the SRD-5M Kvant rangefinding radar; the Type SK-1 ejection seat (4); the internal NR-30 cannon (15); and the Tumansky R-11F-300 two-shaft afterburning turbojet engine (8). (István Toperczer Collection)

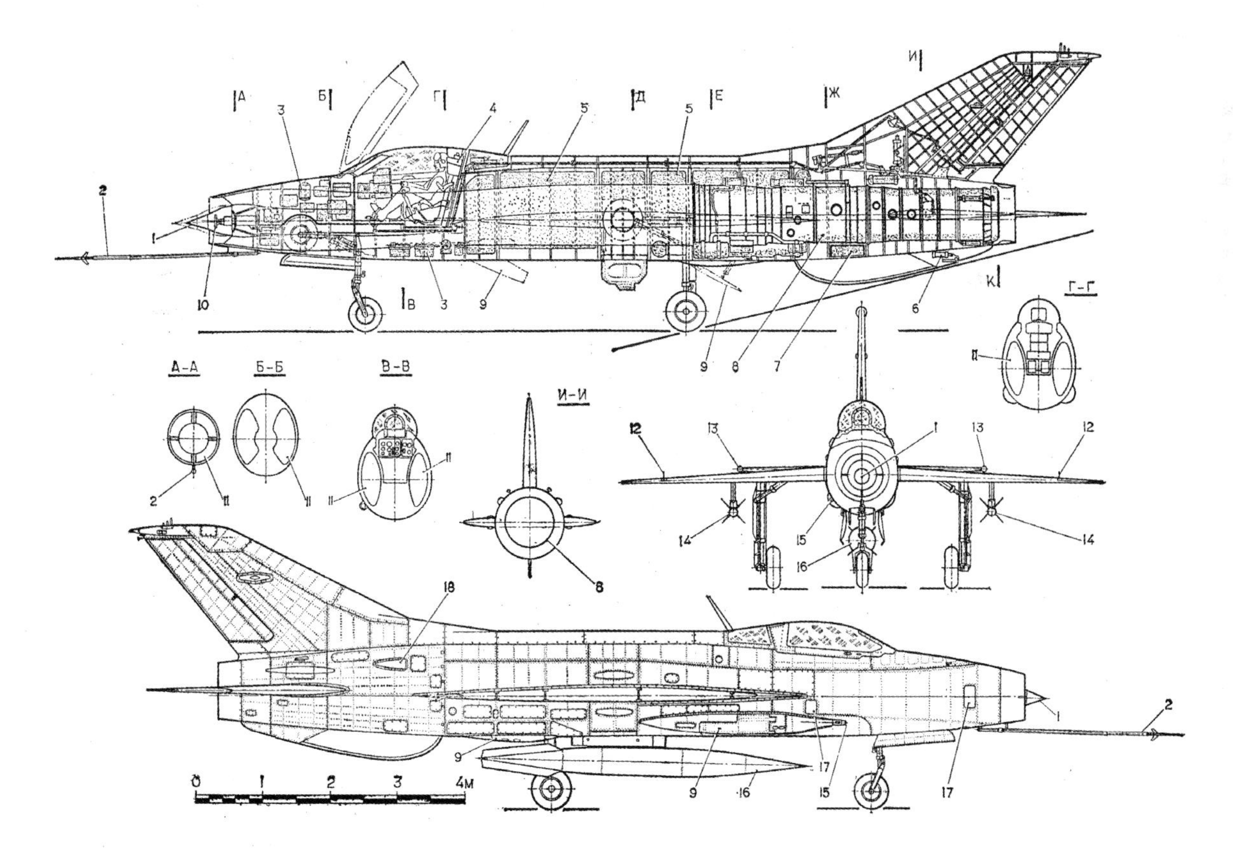

As development progressed, the wing fences were reduced to two smaller examples, and two 30mm NR-30 guns, each fed by a 30-round belt, were added. The third Ye-6 tested the centerline fuel tank, which added 400 miles to the aircraft's range at altitude.

In late 1958, research center OKB-134 was told to produce a copy of an American GAR-9 (later redesignated the AIM-9B) Sidewinder missile – an intact example of the latter had recently been acquired from China as a misfired trophy after scraps between communist MiG-17s and Nationalist Chinese F-86 Sabres off the coast of Taiwan. The copy, dubbed R-3S (NATO code name AA-2 "Atoll"), was ready for testing in February 1959, and Ye-6/2 was modified to carry two on wingtip launchers. Poor test results changed their location to the two underwing hardpoints on APU-13 launchers. This simple armament configuration at least made for quick turnaround times – an early MiG-21 could be rearmed and have its fuel topped up within ten minutes.

The third prototype Ye-6/3 masqueraded as the "Ye-66" and established world records for absolute speed (October 1959) and 100km closed circuit speed (September 1960), reaching a maximum speed of 1,556mph. For production MiG-21s, the possibility of attaining Mach 2 was severely curtailed by the aircraft's limited fuel capacity.

Based on the Ye-6T, the MiG-21F ("F" for *Forsazh* or "boosted") entered production in 1958 at *Gosudarstvennyi Aviatsionnyi Zavod* (GAZ – State Aircraft Factory) 21 in the industrial city of Gorky, with the first deliveries of 40 aircraft made in the autumn of 1959. The MiG-21F had a three-pole SRO-2M "Odd Rods" IFF antenna on top of the vertical fin and a second antenna on the fuselage underside just behind the nosewheel bay. The aircraft was equipped with an ASP-5ND gunsight and an SRD-5 "High Fix" radar range finder, and was armed with two Nudelman-Rikhter NR-30 30mm cannon with 60 rounds of ammunition per gun. It lacked underwing missile pylons, however. Like early variants of many aircraft, this was the lightest, simplest, and most easily flown MiG-21 model of them all. As extra equipment and, consequently, weight were added to later versions, it became harder to handle.

The MiG-21F-13 "Fishbed-C" was the first version to be built in substantial numbers. Early examples were similar to the MiG-21F, but with the left cannon removed to accommodate guidance equipment for two R-3S missiles. The latter were carried on underwing pylons that had been reinstalled and modified to also carry rocket pods, small bombs, or air-to-ground rockets. Late-build MiG-21F-13s were optimized for the daylight interception mission, being equipped with a nose-mounted SRD-5M Kvant (NATO codename "Scan Fix") rangefinding radar and powered by a Tumansky R-11F-300 twin-shaft afterburning turbojet engine producing 12,650lb st thrust.

The MiG-21F-13 was built exclusively for the VVS at GAZ 21 between 1960–62, after which production shifted to the Znamya Truda factory (GAZ 30) in Moscow, where all export MiG-21F-13s were produced between 1962–65.

Mikoyan-Gurevich extensively redesigned the MiG-21F-13 for its second-generation variants, with the modifications made being aimed at extending the fighter's somewhat limited endurance and giving the aircraft a better all-weather capability through the installation of an upgraded radar system.

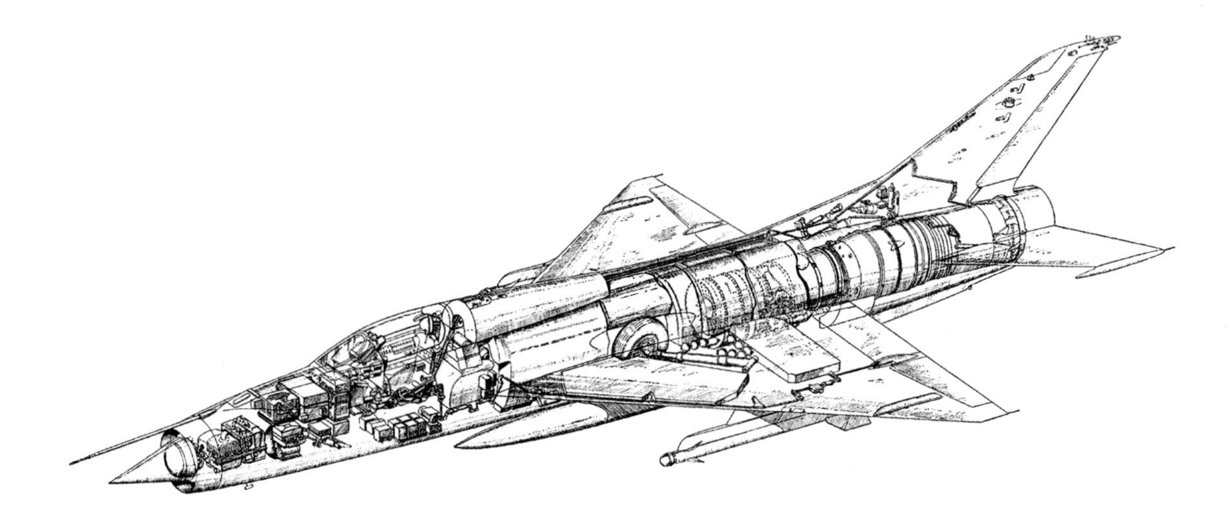

Although not annotated like the artwork of the MiG-21F-13, this cutaway of a MiG-21PF (included in the manual for the "Fishbed-D") reveals the aircraft's key elements. These include the RP-21 Sapfir radar housed in the nose, the Type SK-1 ejection seat, wing pylon-mounted APU-13 rail launchers for the K-13 (R-3S) AAMs and the Tumansky R-11F2-300 afterburning turbojet engine. (István Toperczer Collection)

Later "Fishbeds" were also representative of the trend toward dedicated missile-carrying fighters that lacked internal cannon armament.

In June 1960 a small preproduction series was built under the designation MiG-21P. The MiG-21PF (*Perekhvatchik Forsazh*, or Interceptor Boosted) "Fishbed-D" was basically a MiG-21P with a more powerful 13,640lb st Tumansky R-11F2-300 afterburning turbojet engine and a modified jet exhaust. Within its enlarged and lengthened nose intake, the TsD-30TP radar was replaced by an improved RP-21 Sapfir (NATO codename "Spin Scan") intercept radar, while in the cockpit, the ASP-5ND gunsight made way for the PKI-1 collimator gunsight. The sole remaining 30mm cannon was deleted so as to preserve the center of gravity, and armament restricted to air-to-air missiles (AAMs) and air-to-ground stores on the two wing pylons.

Late-production MiG-21PFs had an extension of the fin's leading edge to reduce yaw. A frequent problem afflicting supersonic aircraft, yaw could cause an engine stall if the jet was turned too abruptly at high speed.

The MiG-21PFV was a "tropicalized" version of the MiG-21PF exclusively produced for the VPAF at GAZ 30, with examples being specially prepared for the hot and humid climate of Southeast Asia. Although the MiG-21PFV was externally similar to a standard VVS MiG-21PF, it was fitted with the less sophisticated R-2L version of the RP-21 radar. This led to the VPAF giving the fighter the designation MiG-21PFL. Production of the MiG-21PF for the VVS commenced in 1962 at GAZ 21 and ended in 1964. The entire production line was then moved to GAZ 30, which continued to build aircraft for export customers until 1968.

The MiG-21PFM (*Modifikatsirovanny* – Modified) "Fishbed-F" was effectively an improved MiG-21PF, this new variant featuring a fixed windscreen and hinged main canopy that opened to starboard in place of the forward-opening single-piece canopy of previous models. The SK-1 ejection seat was replaced by a more advanced zero-zero KM-1 ejection seat. The PFM had an even broader fin, with a brake parachute fairing in the fin root. In earlier MiG-21s the parachute had been stored in the bottom section of the rear fuselage, which meant it could only be deployed after touchdown.

The new, elevated location allowed it to be released earlier, thus drastically reducing the landing distance of the MiG-21PFM.

A further improvement was the introduction of "blown" flaps, which were also fitted to late-production MiG-21PFs – such aircraft were designated MiG-21PF-SPSs (also known as MiG-21PFSs). Bleed air from the engine's compressor section was channeled over the upper flap surfaces, when they were lowered, and this dramatically improved the "Fishbed's" takeoff and landing characteristics. The Tumansky engine adopted from the MiG-21PF was modified for use with the blown flap system, the powerplant being designated R-11F2S-300. Although the MiG-21PFM was not equipped with an internal gun, it was possible to mount a 290kg GP-9 gun pod on the underfuselage centerline. GAZ 21 built MiG-21PFMs for the VVS between 1964–65, while GAZ 30 assembled export MiG-21PFMs between 1966–68.

MiG-21s in North Vietnam

The first batch of MiG-21PFL "Fishbed-Ds" reached North Vietnam in December 1965, with Batch I (bort numbers "4021–4029" and "4120–4124") being handed over through to February 1966, while Batch II (bort numbers "4125–4129," "4220–4229," and "4320–4328") arrived between February 1966 and January 1967. Batches I and II consisted of 34 fighters and four two-seat MiG-21U "Mongol-A" trainers (bort numbers "4123–4124" and "4327–4328").

The disassembled MiG-21PFLs had been shipped in component form in wooden crates aboard Soviet freighters, the vessels docking in Haiphong. Unloaded at night, the crates filled with fuselages and wings were moved by rail in canvas-covered wagons under the cover of darkness to the Yen Vien terminus in Hanoi. The containers were then transferred from there by truck to Noi Bai (also known as Da Phuc), home of the 921st FR. Once at the airfield, VPAF engineers, working day and night under the guidance of Soviet personnel, reassembled the fighters. Following successful test flights by VVS pilots, the MiG-21PFLs were issued to the 921st FR.

Pham Thanh Ngan was flying MiG-21PFL "Red 4128" on October 9, 1966 when his wingman Nguyen Van Minh used S-5M rockets to shoot down F-4B BuNo 152993 from VF-154 over Phu Ly. Its crew, Lt Cdr C. N. Tanner and Lt R. R. Terry, ejected into captivity. Minh's MiG-21 ("Red 4221") was downed by Cdr R. M. Bellinger, CO of F-8E-equipped VF-162, moments later. (István Toperczer Collection)

Small groups of 20–30 Soviet technicians (engineers, propulsion system technicians and airframe, armament and radio specialists) would work at Noi Bai on MiG-21s throughout *Rolling Thunder*. A handful of pilots were also part of this group, undertaking test and training flights. The presence of the latter has led to speculation over the years that Soviet pilots played an active part in combat operations, just as they had done in North Korea 15 years earlier. The VPAF consistently denied that this was the case, as the North Vietnamese leadership was firmly against any kind of direct confrontation of this sort between the superpowers in Southeast Asia.

The primary role of the VVS personnel was to teach their North Vietnamese counterparts how to maintain and fly the MiG-21. In respect to combat operations, they could only give advice, and it was up to the VPAF to decide whether or not to act upon it. Soviet pilots found it relatively easy to converse with their North Vietnamese counterparts since most of them spoke good Russian after years of training at Krasnodar, in the Soviet Union. Some of the groundcrew also spoke Russian, although in the majority of cases an interpreter was required, which routinely led to misunderstandings.

In January 1966 the 921st FR officially declared itself ready for operations with the MiG-21. On the 25th of that month the first R-3S missile-armed "Fishbed-Ds" undertook combat alert duty at the western end of Noi Bai, and in February the aircraft started flying sorties.

On March 4, 1966 VPAF radar units reported the presence of an AQM-34 Firebee reconnaissance drone, and regimental commander Dao Dinh Luyen ordered a MiG-21PFL to readiness. At 1353 hrs a drone was sighted over the Vietnam–Laos border west of Quan Hoa heading for Viet Tri and Bac Can at a speed of 800km/h. Three minutes later another appeared over Vu Ban, east of Hanoi, flying at an altitude of 5,000m in the direction of Thai Nguyen in northeast Vietnam. Future eight-victory MiG-21 ace Nguyen Hong Nhi was scrambled and directed toward one of the drones, which accelerated to beyond Mach 1 (1,235 km/h) and climbed to 17,000m.

When Nhi was 15km away he was ordered to switch on his aircraft's radar. At a range of three kilometers he fired his first R-3S and, 1.5 seconds later, his second. He then broke away. The Firebee was destroyed about 70km northeast of Hanoi while at an altitude in excess of 17,000m. Its destruction represented not only Nhi's first kill but also the first aerial victory to be scored by a VPAF MiG-21.

Cross-sectioned examples of the R-11F-300 engine, as fitted to the MiG-21F-13, were widely employed by Soviet training schools in the instruction of both pilots and groundcrew sent to the USSR. Such aids gave VPAF personnel a better understanding of how the "Fishbed's" turbojet engine operated. The R-11, which had first been bench-tested in early 1956, would become one of the most successful engines of its type ever built – more than 20,900 examples were eventually manufactured. (István Toperczer)

In the wake of combat losses in 1966–67, and following a request from first-generation VPAF pilots who had previously flown MiG-17s, the Soviet Union provided North Vietnam with former Cuban air force MiG-21F-13 "Fishbed-Cs" in the summer and fall of 1967. Although this variant could be armed with two R-3S missiles and had a single NR-30 cannon fitted as standard, it was equipped with the rudimentary SRD-5M Kvant semi-active radar rangefinder that had a range of just 0.5–7km.

MiG-21F-13s in Batch I (bort numbers "4329", "4420–4429," and "4520") were handed over between June–August, while Batch II jets (bort numbers "4521–4529" and "4620–4622") arrived in September–October – a total of 24 fighters and 480 R-3Ss were delivered.

What was soon apparent to the "Fishbed-C" pilots was the aircraft's superiority over the MiG-21PF in respect to its maneuverability at altitudes of between 2,000–6,000m, its tighter turning circle, and higher rate of climb. But it also had weaknesses, specifically its smaller fuel capacity and austere navigational and targeting capabilities due to its primitive semi-active radar-ranging equipment.

MiG-21F-13s started to undertake combat alert duty from July 1967, but it was not until September 16 that a "Fishbed-C" pilot was credited with an aerial victory. VPAF radar had detected the approach of enemy aircraft near Xam Neua, in Laos, and this was followed by reports of two RF-101Cs flying between Nghia Lo and Thanh Son, in RP-6. At 1055 hrs two Noi Bai-based MiG-21F-13s were scrambled to intercept. Shortly afterwards the Voodoos were sighted by Nguyen Ngoc Do and Pham Thanh Ngan flying in step formation at an altitude of 5,500m some eight kilometers away.

After the RF-101C pilots had finished taking their photographs of the northwest railway line, they began to exit the area, climbing to an altitude of 7,315m. Do and Ngan increased their speed to Mach 1.4 and climbed to 6,000m, at which point the former claimed to have shot down Capt R. E. Patterson's Voodoo with an R-3S. Ngan also fired a missile, striking Maj B. R. Bagley's aircraft over Son La. Both RF-101Cs were assigned to the 432nd Tactical Reconnaissance Wing's 20th Tactical Reconnaissance Squadron, and USAF records attributed the loss of Patterson's jet to AAA. Do's victory made him the VPAF's first MiG-21 ace.

The following month, the Soviet Union agreed to provide North Vietnam with MiG-21PFM "Fishbed-Fs," and the first example arrived via ship at Haiphong harbor in December 1967. Their delivery coincided with the return home of 33 newly-graduated "Fishbed" pilots from Krasnodar, and many of these aviators would fly the 36 MiG-21PFMs supplied to the VPAF.

During 1967 and through to mid-1968, MiG-21F-13s and MiG-21PFLs shouldered the burden against USAF and US Navy combat aircraft, but during the second half of 1968 the "Fishbed-F" became the VPAF's primary fighter.

The MiG-21PFM had, in fact, claimed its first aerial victory as early as January 3, 1968. On that date, the 921st FR scrambled two jets from Noi Bai after a large formation of enemy aircraft was detected by radar in the northwest region. Nguyen Dang Kinh ("Red 5018") and Bui Duc Nhu ("Red 5030") headed for Thanh Son, where the former spotted bomb-laden F-105s flying ahead of escorting F-4s. He immediately launched an R-3S that he claimed hit a Thunderchief. Nhu quickly followed suit, shooting down a second F-105 at very close range. Neither loss was confirmed by official USAF records, however. Upon landing at Kep airfield, Kinh overran the runway and destroyed his nose landing gear. Further damage was caused to the cockpit when the groundcrew were forced to smash the canopy in order to extricate the uninjured pilot.

USAF fighter-bombers returned several hours later when 36 aircraft were reported flying over Yen Chau, heading for the Kinh No railway marshaling yard. During the ensuing battle, Ha Van Chuc ("Red 5030") shot down Col J. E. Bean's 469th TFS/388th TFW F-105D west of Thai Nguyen.

MiG Bases

MiG-21 operations were routinely undertaken from Noi Bai, Kep, and Gia Lam during *Rolling Thunder*, these bases having been developed in the wake of MoD resolution 15/QDA, dated 3 March, 1955, which saw an Airfield Research Committee established with the aim of operating the existing facilities inherited from the French and helping the General Staff create an air force. Dang Tinh was made head of the committee in May 1955, when its primary tasks were to take over existing airfields and carry out any repairs that were deemed necessary to return them to operational order.

At this time, four airfields played an important role in the development of military aviation in North Vietnam – Cat Bi, Kien An, Gia Lam, and Do Son. The first restoration work undertaken by the committee in the final months of 1955 saw the runways extended and hangars repaired at Gia Lam and Cat Bi. By January 1959 a network of airfields had been established in North Vietnam, with rudimentary bases south of Hanoi at Gia Lam, Vinh, and Dong Hoi, in the northwest at Na San, Dien Bien, Lai Chau, and Lao Cai, in the northeast at Cat Bi, Kien An, Do Son, and Tien Yen, and in the north at Lang Son and Cao Bang.

In order to boost the defense of Hanoi, construction of Noi Bai airfield was commenced on May 1, 1960. The VPAF was fully aware of its importance, and Chinese engineers were called in to oversee the building of the base. Each day, more than 10,000 laborers toiled away on its construction using materials delivered by 200 trucks. By mid-1964 the main structures of the airfield had been completed, thus allowing the first MiG-17s to be flown in from China on 6 August.

In May 1965 vice Prime Minister Le Thanh Nghi ordered the MoD to build airfields at Yen Bai, Hoa Lac, Kep, and Tho Xuan and expand Gia Lam and Kien An – work on the latter two bases was completed by the end of 1965.

Tran Hanh (left), deputy regiment commander of the 921st FR, briefs his newly trained colleagues (from left to right, unknown, Nguyen Cat A, Nguyen Van Coc, Nguyen Van Minh, Nguyen Van Ly, Mai Van Cuong and Pham Thanh Ngan) at Noi Bai shortly after their return to North Vietnam from the USSR. They are all wearing VKK-4 high-altitude compensating flightsuits and GSh-4 helmets – a combination not often seen once these men commenced combat operations. (István Toperczer Collection)

MiG-21s from the 921st FR and MiG-17s from the 923rd FR operated side-by-side from Noi Bai during *Rolling Thunder*. This aerial view of the airfield, taken by a USAF reconnaissance aircraft, shows six "Fishbeds" and five "Fresco-Cs" sharing earth revetments at Noi Bai in late 1967. These revetments had been hastily constructed after American aircraft started targeting VPAF airfields following the implementation of the "in the nest" tactic from October 1967. (István Toperczer Collection)

Direct attacks by American aircraft on VPAF airfields were sporadic in 1965–66, although they became more frequent from April 1967 once the bases had been removed from the restricted list by the US government. By the summer of that year six airfields were deemed suitable for fighter operations – Noi Bai, Gia Lam, Kep, Hoa Lac, Kien An and Tho Xuan.

As part of a drive to increase the effectiveness of the fighter force, senior VPAF officers eventually decided that a solitary MiG-17 or MiG-21 should be in the air at all times, and to achieve this a taxiway at Noi Bai was also used as a second runway. Although this presented a problem for "Fishbed" pilots due to the short length of the taxiway, it also gave them something of an advantage as US intelligence believed Noi Bai did not possess a second runway long enough to facilitate MiG-21 operations.

In October 1967 the US strategy in respect to the communist fighter threat changed following an increasing number of losses to MiGs over North Vietnam. Now, every effort would be made to paralyze VPAF operations through the implementation of the so-called "in the nest" tactic – hitting aircraft on the ground at their bases. Noi Bai would be attacked on nine separate occasions that month and Kep no fewer than 29 times.

In the immediate aftermath of these strikes, the civilian population in Vinh Phu Province and groundcrew from the 921st FR tried to return Noi Bai to operational status. Only one primary radar unit (some five kilometers from the airfield) remained active, with secondary back-up sites being situated up to ten kilometers away. Additional coverage was also provided by sites even further afield. Contact between these units was maintained via radio, telephone, and courier.

Following the attacks, the fighter regiments at the targeted bases relocated their stores to shelters more than ten kilometers away, and petrol and jet fuel was trucked to airfields depending on daily operational requirements, rather than being being stored on-site.

Although Noi Bai had to be evacuated after the fifth attack in October 1967, American fighter-bombers returned six times in November and seven in December. During the course of air strikes on Noi Bai, Kep, Kien An, and Hoa Lac airfields between January 1967 and March 1968, 17 aircraft, three helicopters, and numerous fuel trucks, buildings, and runways were destroyed. In 50 percent of the raids, the target airfield would be put out of action – sometimes for just a few hours, but on a number of occasions for several days. In all, these four airfields were rendered inoperable on 36 separate occasions for a total of 120 days over a period of 15 months.

Due to the increasing number of attacks on airfields, the government agreed to a request from the MoD and the VPAF that individual provinces should be ordered to repair damaged bases. The effort required to reopen Noi Bai, Kep, Kien An, and Gia Lam airfields took the equivalent of 200,000 working days to complete, with 70 percent of the work being carried out by civilians. A total of 140 earth shelters for aircraft were also built, these usually being positioned between 500–2,000m from the runway, although sometimes they were located as far as 3,000m away. The concrete taxiways from the shelters were 20m wide, and they could also serve as runways.

Finally, MiG bunkers were dug into nearby hills at Noi Bai, Yen Bai, Anh Son, and Kien An. Boasting camouflaged armored double concrete doors, they could accommodate betwen six and 30 MiGs. When the scramble order came, the "Fishbeds" started up in the bunkers and then took off either from a taxiway or runway. Underground command and control centers were also constructed, along with shelters for support equipment.

Following the first bombing raids in the wake of this construction work, it was immediately apparent that the open earth shelters provided protection against standard conventional high-explosive ordnance but not against cluster bomb-type sub-munitions. A number of them were quickly "enhanced" with the addition of pitched roofs – these shelters looked like normal huts when seen from the air. However, their roofs were made from rails and steel plates used in runway construction, with soil then piled on top and covered in turf. The size of the "enhanced" shelters was based on the dimensions of a MiG-21, being 15m long, 10m wide, and 7m high, and using up 30–35 rails and 300 plates.

Following the loss of several MiGs on the ground during the airfield bombing campaign in the fall of 1967, the VPAF decided that it had to disperse its valuable fighters to safer locations some distance from operational bases. Soviet technicians quickly developed a special harness and cables that allowed aircraft weighing up to eight tons to be slung beneath an Mi-6 "Hook" helicopter. A fully-fueled and armed MiG-17 or an empty MiG-19 or MiG-21 could then be flown to newly built mountain caves some 30km from the Hanoi airfields. Once back on the ground, the aircraft was pushed into its underground hangar by truck. The transportation of MiGs for maintenance, dispersal, and operational tasks was undertaken by the VPAF's handful of Mi-6s on more than 400 occasions without any major accidents.

Ground defenses surrounding all airfields were also drastically improved, with AAA and SAM sites quickly proliferating. The three most heavily defended bases were Noi Bai, Gia Lam, and Kien An, each of which was protected by seven 100mm AAA batteries, four 57mm AAA batteries, BTR-40 mobile flak platforms, and an SA-2 SAM regiment.

The first MiG-21PFM ("Red 5001") delivered to the VPAF is flown into Noi Bai slung beneath an Mi-6 "Hook" helicopter in late 1967. A special harness was designed for carrying MiG-21s between the underground hangars cut into mountainsides and their nearby operating airfields. This happened more than 400 times during the war. (István Toperczer Collection)

CHAPTER 3
PATH TO COMBAT

Pilots and engineers assigned specifically to the MiG-21 had been sent to the Soviet Union for training as early as April 1965, whilst MiG-17 pilots who had trained in the USSR from 1961 to 1964, as well as selected 921st FR "Fresco" pilots already serving in the frontline, also commenced their "Fishbed" conversion training at this time. Whilst in the Soviet Union, they flew a variety of types at the Krasnodar Flight Officers' School. After an initial language course, students embarked on the study of up to 20 theoretical subjects that included aerodynamics, meteorology, aircraft construction, weapons systems, avionics, navigation, and combat tactics.

Their flying training started on the Yak-18, and after completing 100 flying hours they moved on to the two-seat MiG-15UTI in the second year, before graduating to the MiG-17 in the third year. During their 150 hours of flying in the "Fresco," students were instructed in simple aerobatics, route flying, basic aerial combat, and ground attack. When undertaking the latter, cadets were occasionally cleared to fire the cannon in the MiG-15UTI or MiG-17. Once a year students used an ejection seat simulator and biannually they made parachute jumps from an An-2. The training syllabus was changed in 1966 when L-29 Delfins replaced Yak-18s at Primorsko-Akhtarsk. Students had to complete 80 flying hours in the Czech-built jet trainer before moving on to the MiG-15UTI and MiG-17 to log a further 40 hours on each type.

North Vietnamese cadets look over a MiG-21PF at Krasnodar airfield, prior to flying the aircraft for the first time. They would use the more austere PFL variant of the "Fishbed-D" once they had returned home. (István Toperczer Collection)

Pilots who graduated from the first MiG-21 course at Krasnodar had logged an impressive 400–500 flying hours by the time they were declared operational with the 921st FR. However, because of the pressing need for "Fishbed" pilots, those that completed subsequent courses had only 250–300 flying-hours in their logbooks prior to reaching the frontline.

VPAF student pilots are briefed by their Soviet instructors in front of L-29 Delfins at Primorsko-Akhtarsk in May 1966. The aircraft were assigned to the Krasnodar Flight Officers' School in the Soviet Union, where VPAF cadets flew a minimum of 80 hours in the Delfin prior to moving on to the MiG-21. (István Toperczer Collection)

The VPAF cadets of the Flight Training Squadrons (known as "Doans") destined to fly the MiG-21 during *Rolling Thunder* were trained on three main courses, two of them at Krasnodar (1965–66/Doans 3 and 4, and 1965–68/Doans 6 and 7) and one in North Vietnam (1966/Doans 1 and 2). The second Soviet-based MiG-21 pilot training course, which commenced in mid-1965, saw student pilots accompanied by two groups of 300 engineers who were there for technical training. From June of that year, 20 cadets of Doan 6, led by Pham Dinh Tuan, received instruction on the Yak-18, MiG-17, and MiG-21. In July, an additional 59 students of Doan 7, led by Dinh Ton, commenced training on the L-29 Delfin in the first year, before progressing to the MiG-17 and MiG-21. Only 13 cadets from Doan 7 subsequently flew the "Fishbed" operationally.

The growing demands of the escalating war at home meant that pilots were required as a matter of urgency. From 1966, cadets had only three months to learn the Russian language – their predecessors on the first MiG-21 course had had a year. After the first year of L-29 flying, no fewer than 39 cadets were excluded because of their poor physical condition or lack of flying aptitude. The most talented 36 progressed to the MiG-21, while 44 students remained with the MiG-17. Later, three more were also moved to the less demanding "Fresco."

As these numbers clearly show, the VPAF cadets were severely tested by their Soviet instructors. The latter only allowed them to participate in the final stages of flight training once the cadets were graded as both mentally and physically fit following a series of closely scrutinized evaluation flights. The training program for the North Vietnamese was shorter and progressed at a faster pace than for their Soviet counterparts, and the syllabus became even more compressed from 1966 onward. The drop-out rate was very high, and sometimes only 20 out of 100 students made it to flight status, with the rest becoming groundcrew. Amongst the few to make the cut from the first MiG-21 course was Nguyen Van Coc:

> My group numbered 120 students at the start of the course. After completing studies in flight theory, only 60 cadets were left and, eventually, just eight MiG-17 and eight MiG-21 pilots were qualified. The Soviet instructors were extremely good but very tough, which meant that we needed to learn fast. We were

thoroughly trained by pilots who knew their stuff at Krasnodar, which meant we were fully prepared for combat operations by the time we completed the course on the MiG-21. This in turn meant that a number of us subsequently became aces.

All North Vietnamese students had to "ride" the L-29 ejection seat simulator at Primorsko-Akhtarsk during their training course. This purpose-built rig allowed them to practice the procedures leading up to a successful ejection without them running the risk of suffering spinal injuries. Most VPAF MiG-21 pilots were forced to abandon their aircraft at least once during combat, with a number experiencing multiple ejections. (István Toperczer Collection)

Coc returned to Vietnam in mid-May 1966 and joined the 921st FR, claiming his first aerial success 11 months later.

Another graduate of the second course was future ace Nguyen Van Nghia, who recalled:

In September 1965 I started my course at Primorsko-Akhtarsk, near the Sea of Azov, the city's airfield being operated by the Krasnodar Flight Officers' School. The first aircraft I trained on was the L-29 Delfin, which I flew alongside the Yak-18. At the completion of the first course I had 180 hours on the L-29 and had made 15 flights with the instructor before my first solo on the jet. The school then chose 24 of us from the 60 student pilots to see if we could go straight to the MiG-21 from the L-29, skipping the MiG-17. I was among those selected. Eventually, 21 of the 24 student pilots succeeded in flying the MiG-21.

We enjoyed a 20-day holiday in Sochi, on the Black Sea, after finishing our L-29 course. Upon our return to flight school we started with classroom lectures on the theory behind flying the MiG-21, before going back to Primorsko-Akhtarsk for 20 more hours on the L-29. This increased my total flying time on the Delfin to 200 hours. We returned to Krasnodar for the MiG-21 flying program, and I logged another 56 flying hours. When I'd completed my training in the Soviet Union I had 256 flying hours in my logbook.

Before we returned home, Vu Ngoc Dinh from the group of older pilots and my commanding officer, Nguyen Hong Nhi, came to brief us on the aerial battles being fought over Vietnam so that we could practice more effectively in the remaining time we had. We didn't have much information about the enemy. Dinh and Nhi just told us about typical combats, and not the characteristics of the American aircraft we would be fighting.

By the time Coc and Nghia returned to North Vietnam and joined the 921st FR, the unit was being led by MiG-17 pilots who had been successful in the earlier aerial battles, namely Dao Dinh Luyen, Tran Manh, Tran Hanh, and Pham Ngoc Lan, who became unit and flight commanders within the 921st following its re-equipment with MiG-21s. These Chinese-trained "Fresco" pilots, along with Nguyen Nhat Chieu, Nguyen Ngoc Do, and Le Trong Huyen, had commenced their MiG-21 conversion course with the 921st FR

During the mid-1960s, Hungarian and North Vietnamese cadets undertook identical flying training courses in the Soviet Union. Here, László Reindl poses for a group photograph with fellow cadets from the VPAF, several of whom subsequently claimed victories in the defense of North Vietnam. Standing in the back row are, from left to right, Nguyen Van Ly, Nguyen Kim Tu, Vu Ngoc Dinh, To Nhat Bai, and Phan Thanh Tinh, and in the front row, again from left to right, are Nguyen Ba Dich, Nguyen Van Thuan, and László Reindl. (István Toperczer Collection)

in Vietnam in 1966. Luyen's successor as unit commander, Tran Manh, also joined the program at this time, as did future aces Pham Thanh Ngan, Nguyen Hong Nhi, Nguyen Dang Kinh, and Vu Ngoc Dinh. The latter remembered his training in the Soviet Union:

> We received tuition from excellent Russian instructor pilots who never forced us to do things in a specific way. When problem solving, they provided us with numerous options so that we could choose the best one for us. This taught us to think for ourselves, rather than slavishly following our instructors. We were encouraged to be independent thinkers in respect to learning flight theory and fighter tactics and strategies. Having said that, our flight preparation was closely observed by instructors to ensure we stuck to a strict set of rules that were there for our own safety. These related specifically to navigation around Primorsko-Akhtarsk. We needed to be thoroughly familiar with the region surrounding the base to the point where we could mentally picture the landscape and its key features – rivers, roads, mountains, cities etc. – for literally hundreds of kilometers in our mind's eye. We also had to memorize the relevant details of the surrounding airports – their sizes, the takeoff/landing direction of their runway(s), and Morse code signal and radio frequency of their air traffic control centers.
>
> I had been sent to the Soviet Union in 1962 as part of Flight Training Squadron No. 4, being schooled there as a teenager. When I returned home in early 1966, my family was unaware that I was a pilot. All they knew was that I had studied in the Soviet Union. All of our letters home went via the General Politics Bureau, and it took three to four months for correspondence to reach our families. We were instructed not to divulge what we were being taught in the Soviet Union.

In February 1968, as students from the final Krasnodar MiG-21 course neared the completion of their training, four of them (Dinh Ton, Pham Phu Thai,

921st FR pilots familiarize themselves with the take-off characteristics of the MiG-21PFL during a classroom session at Noi Bai following their return from the Soviet Union. (István Toperczer Collection)

Ha Quang Hung, and Luong The Phuc) were urgently flown back to North Vietnam as attrition replacements for three "Fishbed" pilots lost in recent weeks. The remaining 29 continued their training, logging 40 flying hours in the MiG-21PFM and MiG-21US "Mongol-B" trainer. To ensure graduation, they had to pass a series of examinations, both in the classroom and in the air, and, finally, expend R-3S missiles at a variety of different targets. With the completion of these tests, the pilots returned home in mid-1968 and joined the 921st FR.

The two MiG-21 main training courses for the VPAF at the Krasnodar Flight Officers' School in 1965–68 produced 53 pilots, with a further eight receiving tuition in North Vietnam.

The student pilot of MiG-21UM "Mongol-B" "Blue 36" is given clearance to commence taxiing at Krasnodar. VPAF cadets were expected to complete at least 40 hours of flying in the MiG-21 before being declared operational on the type. (István Toperczer Collection)

CHAPTER 4
WEAPON OF WAR

Although the MiG-21 had a performance envelope that rivaled the F-4 Phantom II and exceeded all other American fighter types bar the F-8 Crusader in Southeast Asia during *Rolling Thunder*, the "Fishbed" was so modestly armed in comparison with its rivals that pilots dubbed the early PF and PFM variants the *"Golub Mira"* ("Peace Dove").

The MiG-21s supplied to the VPAF from late 1965 through to the spring of 1968 could carry two R-3S/K-13 (AA-2 "Atoll") infrared-homing or RS-2US/K-5MS (AA-1 "Alkali") semi-active radar-homing AAMs. Each missile was attached to a single BDZ-60-21U underwing pylon fitted with an APU-13M launcher for the R-3S and an APU-7 for the RS-2US. The missiles could be replaced by two UB-16-57 rocket pods housing 16 S-5 series 57mm folding-fin rockets.

Only the 24 MiG-21F-13s acquired by the VPAF in the summer of 1967 featured cannon armament in the form of a single NR-30 30mm weapon mounted internally on the starboard underside of the fuselage. The PFLs and PFMs supplied to the North Vietnamese lacked the centerline mounting seen on later MiG-21 variants (specifically the MF, supplied to the VPAF from December 1971) that could take the weight of a gun pod housing the very effective Gryasev-Shipunov twin-barrel 23mm GSh-23 cannon aimed through an ASP-PF-21 gunsight and giving five seconds of firing time (200 rounds).

The NR-30 installed in the "Fishbed-C" had the potential to be a highly potent weapon thanks to its considerable muzzle velocity and 60-round magazine. However, no MiG-21F-13 pilots were ever officially credited with hitting enemy aircraft with cannon fire, despite US records stating that three F-105s were struck within a 48-hour period on April 28–29, 1967.

On April 28, Capt F. A. Caras of the 44th TFS/388th TFW was flying F-105D 58-1151 as part of "Lightning" flight on a strike against Hanoi's railway repair workshops. After delivering their ordnance, Caras and his wingman were at 3,700m heading for Thailand when both aircraft were hit by R-3Ss fired by two MiG-21s 130km west of Hanoi. The wingman's aircraft

The MiG-21F-13's NR-30 30mm cannon was semi-recessed into the right lower fuselage. A large gun blast panel was mounted on the fuselage around the muzzle, while heated gases produced when the weapon was fired were vented from the gun through slots in the fairing that covered the cannon. Finally, an "airflow relief" door was located above the NR-30 fairing. (István Toperczer)

was only slightly damaged (by what he claimed was cannon fire) but Capt Caras's jet crashed 24km miles east of Na San and he was killed. A number of "Fishbeds" had been airborne that day in response to the attack on Hanoi, as Vu Ngoc Dinh recalled:

> During the afternoon of April 28, 921st FR CO Tran Manh ordered Nguyen Hong Nhi and I to take off and fly to a holding area over Tuyen Quang Province. We did not encounter any enemy aircraft, however, so we returned to Noi Bai. Later, Le Trong Huyen and Dong Van Son were ordered to Combat Alert Condition 1, before being scrambled shortly thereafter to intercept American aircraft approaching from the Tuyen Quang sector. Again, neither pilot successfully engaged enemy aircraft in this area. As they were returning to Noi Bai, a target was suddenly detected on radar south of Son Duong. The command post GCI ordered the flight to turn back to intercept the enemy aircraft, but by the time they had reached the area the contact was too far away for our pilots to attack, so they too landed back at Noi Bai.
>
> A third flight of MiG-21s, flown by Dang Ngoc Ngu and Mai Van Cuong, then took off and headed for the northern slopes of the Tam Dao mountain range. When they were 15km north of Son Duong they turned to port to intercept F-105s fleeing Vietnamese airspace after attacking the railway repair workshop in Hanoi. Both pilots succeeded in bouncing the Thunderchiefs without being seen, Ngu having spotted the jets at a range of four kilometers. Accelerating in pursuit, he fired an R-3S that damaged his target. Cuong, who had remained close to Ngu to cover his leader's attack, saw two more aircraft off to the right and quickly latched onto the tail of Caras's F-105. He also fired an "Atoll," which brought the Thunderchief down.
>
> Following their "hit-and-run" attack, Ngu and Cuong pulled up into a climb to break off the engagement and then returned to base.

The clash on April 29 was detailed in *Red Baron Reports Vol. III*, which was compiled by the Institute for Defense Analyses Systems Evaluation Division of Arlington, Virginia, for the Pentagon based on official combat accounts from USAF and US Navy units. That day, a flight of four F-105Ds (again using the call-sign"Lightning," which presumably meant they too were from the 44th TFS/388th TFW) were assigned the flak suppression role in advance of a strike force attacking a bridge in Hanoi.

After hitting their target, "Lightning 1" and "2" broke away from the flight in an ultimately unsuccessful pursuit of two MiG-17s, while "Lightning 3" and "4" spotted an unidentified silver aircraft as it flew out of cloud cover about three kilometers behind them and off to their left. Both F-105 pilots immediately turned left into the pursuing aircraft, which they identified as a

MiG-21F-13 CANNON ARMAMENT

The MiG-21F-13's sole internal weapon was a single Nudelman-Rikhter NR-30 30mm cannon, which fired a massive projectile. The latter meant that the weapon had to be fitted with a muzzle brake and an integrated flame damper to prevent airframe damage when the cannon was fired. The NR-30 weighed 65kg and fired 410gram shells at a velocity of 780m per second and at a rate of fire of 850–1,000 cycles per minute. The "Fishbed-C's" magazine was typically loaded with 60 high-explosive fragmentation shells for the NR-30. Because of the weapon's heavy caliber, the NR-30 was capable of downing most enemy aircraft with only one or two direct hits.

"clean MiG-21 lacking any AAMs." Although they were initially able to force their opponent to overshoot, the MiG-21 pilot then executed a barrel roll and, despite "Lightning 3" and "4" trying to unload so that they could then turn and accelerate away in afterburner, he gained a firing position.

At an altitude of 3,000m, "Lightning 4" saw his opponent closing on "Lightning 3" and then open fire with his cannon. The lead Thunderchief was shot down and "Lightning 4" damaged before the "Fishbed" broke off its attack. "Lightning 4" spotted the MiG-21 several times over the next few minutes, but its pilot did mount another attack presumably because he had exhausted his ammunition. "Lightning 3" reported that unlike previous VPAF fighters he had encountered, the pilot of this MiG-21 had used his superior speed and maneuverability to press home his attack.

VPAF documentation for April 29, 1967 does not corroborate this action, however, and the only Seventh Air Force loss on that date was an F-4C claimed by ranking MiG-17 ace Nguyen Van Bay and credited to AAA by USAF records. There were no cannon-armed "Fishbeds" in service with the VPAF at this time, for the ex-Cuban MiG-21F-13s were not declared operational until July 1967.

"Alkali"

With all but a relative handful of VPAF MiG-21s lacking cannon during *Rolling Thunder*, pilots had to rely exclusively on the pair of AAMs carried by their "Fishbed D/Fs" when it came to downing enemy aircraft. In April–May 1966, according to Soviet sources, 14 RS-2US missiles were fired at US aircraft by VPAF MiG-21PFs without recording a single success. During the same period, only five AAMs were seen in flight by US aircrew over North Vietnam. Thanks to the AA-1 "Alkali's" rigid G-load maneuvering restrictions and design deficiencies, none of the radar-homing missiles had been successfully guided to their intended targets.

Nguyen Van Nghia recalled live-fire exercises with the "Alkali" missile while undergoing training in the Soviet Union:

The RS-2US/K-5MS (AA-1 "Alkali") was a 1950s-vintage semi-active radar-homing AAM that was only effective against non-maneuvering targets. It proved to be entirely unsuited to aerial combat over North Vietnam in 1966. (István Toperczer)

During radar beam-guided K-5 live missile shoots, our target was an unmanned aircraft flying at an altitude of 6,000–8,000m. When chasing such a target, the radar beam emitted by the "Fishbed" would shrink into a cone shape centered on the contact. The missile would use its guidance vanes to adjust its course in order to remain in the center of the cone. You had to keep the MiG-21 steady so that the radar beam remained locked on to the target throughout the missile's time in flight until it hit. Achieving a kill with a K-5 was a lot more difficult than with an infrared-guided K-13 "shoot and forget" AAM.

When the missile left its rail, the aircraft jerked upwards and the wings would rock. You also had to look out for exhaust efflux from the missile's jet motor being ingested into the engine intake, as this could cause the R-11 to stall. Finally, if an AAM was fired at close quarters to the enemy, the MiG could be struck by debris from the target aircraft when it was hit. You also ran the risk of colliding with your target during such an encounter, as its contact icon disappeared from the radar screen when you were so close.

Development of the RS-2US (K-5) had commenced in 1951, and the weapon entered service as the Grushin/Tomashevich RS-2U (also known as the R-5MS or K-5MS) six years later. Examples of the K-5 AAM were first seen being carried under the wings of Su-9 "Fishpot" all-weather interceptors participating in a flypast of Tushino airfield, in northwest Moscow, during Soviet Air Fleet Day on July 9, 1961.

The 1950s-vintage radar-homing AAM had originally been designed for use with the RP-2U Izumrud-2 (NATO codename "Scan Odd") air-intercept radar installed in the MiG-19PM "Farmer-E", and it was only effective against non-maneuvering targets. The missile proved very sensitive to the shape of the radar beam emitted by the launch aircraft, as well as the movements of the latter, and it was also prone to signal jamming. Designed primarily as an anti-bomber weapon, the "Alkali" had an effective range at low altitude of just 2–5km, while at high altitude this could be extended to seven kilometers. Its warhead weighed 15.2kg.

Shortly after being chosen for fitment in the Su-9, the TsD-Z0T (RP-21) variant of the TsD-30 radar was also squeezed into the MiG-21PF. In principle, the installation of this system meant that the "Fishbed-D" could also use the RS-2US AAM, which had entered service in late 1958. By then, work had commenced in the Soviet Union on the more effective infrared-guided K-13 missile – a reverse-engineered AIM-9B Sidewinder.

Rockets

Unguided S-5M 57mm folding-fin rockets were also occasionally used as air-to-air weapons by VPAF MiG-21PFLs from the spring of 1966. During combat operations, the leader's aircraft would be armed with two R-3Ss, while his wingman's jet carried a single UB-16-57 rocket pod housing 16 S-5Ms under each wing. Although the rocket was capable of a one-hit kill, the pods were considered to be harder to aim than the NR-30 cannon.

The 57mm rockets could be expended in three modes of fire – "one-salvo," "four-salvo," and "Automatic" (which saw all 16 expended in one go). There was

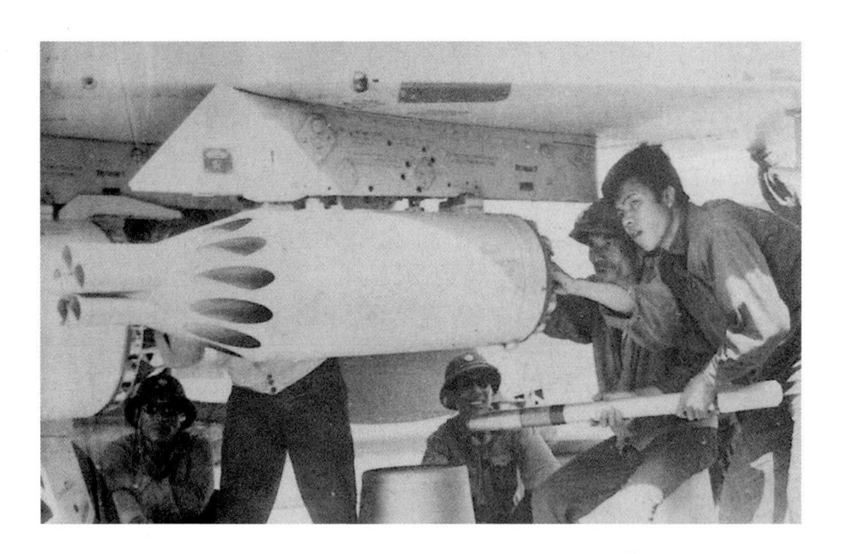

Armorers load a UB-16-57 pod with 16 S-5M 57mm folding-fin rockets. During the air engagements of 1966, the lead "Fishbed" in each pair was equipped with two R-3S AAMs, while the wingman's aircraft carried two rocket pods containing unguided high-explosive fragmentation S-5M rockets. On July 7, 1966, Nguyen Nhat Chieu's wingman, Tran Ngoc Siu, became the first VPAF pilot to enjoy success with the S-5M when he downed F-105D 59-1741 flown by Capt J. H. Tomes of the 354th TFS/355th TFW. USAF loss records attributed Tomes' demise to AAA, however. (István Toperczer Collection)

a 75-microsecond time delay between each rocket firing when "four-salvo" or "Automatic" modes were selected.

The reuseable UB-16-57 pod had been developed by the Soviet Union in 1964 primarily for use in close air support operations against ground area targets, although the VVS also realized that salvoes of S-5s could be effective if fired from close range at tightly packed bomber formations. The pod, which was of all-metal construction and had a conical front-end and a tapering aft section, was mounted on BDZ-60-21D underwing pylons.

The S-5, developed by the Nudelman Precision Engineering Design Bureau as the ARS-57, was inspired by captured examples of the German 55mm R4M Orkan unguided AAM principally used by the Me 262. The rockets were tested in a series of trials by MiG-15bis and MiG-17s through to January 1955, and then accepted into service three months later. Given the military designation S-5, the weapon was produced in a variety of subtypes with different warheads, including the S-5K HEAT (high-explosive anti-tank), S-5M/MO high-explosive fragmentation, and smoke and incendiary rounds. Each rocket was about one meter long, weighed around four kilograms and had a range of 3–4km, depending on warhead and fuze.

According to VPAF sources, a MiG-21 two-ship formation in which the lead jet was armed with two R-3Ss and the wingman's aircraft had a pair of UB-16-57 pods claimed the S-5's first victory over a US aircraft on July 7, 1966. On that day, in response to a USAF attack formation of F-105s from Thailand heading for the railway network in the Thai Nguyen area, MiG-21PFLs flown by future ace Nguyen Nhat Chieu (R-3Ss) and Tran Ngoc Siu (UB-16-57s) were scrambled from Noi Bai. After reaching their briefed operational altitude, they were directed by GCI to patrol over the airfield.

The Thunderchiefs flew along the Tam Dao mountain range and right past Noi Bai, at which point Chieu and Siu commenced their interception. The latter, spotting a flight of F-105s behind him off to his left, informed Chieu and then made a sharp right-hand turn in order to cut in behind two F-105s. Despite the USAF pilots breaking formation, Siu got himself into a favorable position and opened fire from 1,500m. Although the Thunderchief evaded the first salvo of rockets with a tight left turn, two more salvos of S-5Ms fired from as close as 200m hit F-105D 59-1741 (call-sign "Red Eye") in the wing. Chieu saw his wingman's rockets strike the fighter-bomber, causing it to nose over and forcing Capt J. H. Tomes of the 354th TFS/355th TFW to eject. The aircraft crashed 16km northwest of Yen Bai.

Chieu was unable to lock onto a second F-105 that was weaving wildly, and so he did not launch an R-3S. He and Siu then broke away from the remaining

Thunderchiefs before their F-4 escorts had time to react. USAF records state that Tomes' F-105D was hit by 85mm AAA.

Four days later, another rocket attack was made by a 921st FR MiG-21 as described by Vu Ngoc Dinh:

> On July 11, a large number of F-105s escorted by F-4s targeted Vu Chua railway bridge just north of Kep. That day, my MiG-21 was armed with R-3Ss, while the jet flown by my wingman, Dong Van Song, carried two rocket pods. After being scrambled from Noi Bai, we flew two complete circuits over the airfield, and then turned left onto a heading of 310 degrees while flying at an altitude of 2,000m.
>
> We were informed by our command post that the target aircraft were ahead of us at a range of 15km. Song soon told me that he had spotted a flight of F-105s flying below us in the opposite direction. We dropped our auxiliary fuel tanks and increased our speed, ready to employ the "Roll" tactic we had been trained to fly when approaching an enemy formation head-on from above. As we closed

0740 hrs, OCTOBER 9, 1966

PHU LY, HA NAM PROVINCE

1 Scrambled from Noi Bai, two MiG-21PFLs of the 921st FR close in on two flights of F-4Bs from VF-154, embarked in USS *Coral Sea* (CVA-43) operating from *Yankee Station* in the Gulf of Tonkin. The Phantom IIs are climbing as formation leader Pham Thanh Ngan (in "Red 4128") and his wingman Nguyen Van Minh (in "Red 4221") turn hard to the right in order get on to the tails of the enemy fighters.

2 As Ngan prepares to fire his R-3Ss at the lead F-4 in the trailing flight, he sees Minh salvo four S-5M rockets from each of his UB-16-57 pods (one under each wing) at the same jet.

3 Holding fire, Ngan turns away and prepares to cover Minh as he continues his attack.

4 As Minh's rockets hit the lead F-4B (BuNo 152993, flown by Lt Cdr C. N. Tanner and Lt R. R. Terry), he spots another Phantom II bearing down on him from just off his nose and he turns hard into the attack.

5 With Minh having foiled his attack, the pilot of the F-4 breaks hard to the left to escape. Minh uses the high speed of his MiG-21 to close on to the tail of the turning Phantom II and unleashes two more four-rocket salvoes, but they fail to reach their target before the fighter makes good its escape.

6 Minh then spots two more F-4s above him. Closing to within 400m of the enemy jets, he fires eight more rockets and then breaks away before seeing the results of his attack. Again, Minh's S-5Ms fail to hit their target.

7 Unseen by Minh's GCI or Ngan, two low-flying F-8E Crusaders from VF-162, embarked in USS *Oriskany* (CVA-34), spot "Red 4221" and zoom-climb to intercept the VPAF fighter.

8 Seeing the fast-closing Crusaders at the last minute, Minh vainly attempts to evade the pursuing fighters by flying a "split-S" maneuver. The first Sidewinder missile streaks past the MiG-21PFL, but the second runs true. Quickly realizing his burning jet is doomed, Minh successfully ejects. Cdr R. M. Bellinger, in BuNo 149159, has just claimed the first "Fishbed" to fall to a US Navy Crusader.

FOLLOWING PAGES

1
4128
3
5
2
4

6
7
8
4221

> on the target aircraft, the lead pilot called "Roll left or right" and then performed a "split-s" maneuver behind the bandit. The leader and his wingman swapped positions while carrying out the "Roll," resulting in the wingman attacking first with rockets while the leader covered him.
>
> I ordered Song to "Roll right" and he quickly latched on to the tail of an F-105. Song sped forward to a range of 500m and fired two salvos of rockets, but they missed their target. He adjusted his aim and fired a third salvo at a range of 300m. Whilst holding station behind my wingman, I clearly saw the rockets hit one of the F-105s – it began to trail smoke and lose altitude.

Maj William McClelland's F-105D 61-0121 (call-sign "Anvil 2") from the 355th TFW was damaged by Song's rocket fire as it flew over Thai Nguyen, and although the USAF pilot tried to nurse the Thunderchief back to Thailand, he was forced to eject over Laos when the jet ran out of fuel. A USAF HH-3C helicopter from Udorn rescued him shortly thereafter.

As these two engagements had shown, the VPAF initially enjoyed some success with a standard pair of MiG-21s equipped with a mix of weapons. However, some pilots were still unsure as to whether or not they should use R-3Ss or rocket pods when engaging enemy aircraft, while others wanted the Soviet Union to supply cannon-armed variants at a time when all the MiG-21PFLs delivered to the VPAF lacked a centerline GP-9 gun pod.

After analyzing a number of aerial engagements during the second half of 1966, it was decided that all MiG-21s would be armed with R-3Ss rather than having a mix of AAMs and rocket pods. The "Atoll" not only enjoyed a higher rate of success, its carriage did not affect the maneuverablity of the "Fishbed" – the aircraft's G-rating was reduced when carrying UB-16-57s. A number of newly trained MiG-21 pilots flying as wingmen to their more experienced flight leaders also requested that their aircraft be armed with R-3Ss.

"Atoll"

The first "Atolls" had been delivered to the VPAF in early 1966, and initially their supply was very limited. The weapon, built by Vympel as the K-13, was a short-range, infrared-guided AAM developed by the Soviet Union in the late 1950s. It was similar in appearance and function to the American AIM-9B Sidewinder from which it was reverse-engineered.

As previously mentioned, in September 1958, in a series of aerial engagements between Republic of China Air Force F-86Fs and MiG-17Fs of the People's Liberation Army Air Force during the Taiwan Strait Crisis, the Sabre pilots fired six GAR-9s at their opponents and claimed four victories. One Sidewinder launched during a coastal clash misfired and fell intact in Chinese territory, while another AIM-9B hit a MiG-17 (on September 28) but did not explode, the missile becoming embedded within the fuselage of the "Fresco." It was subsequently removed after the jet had landed. The Chinese sent both missiles to Moscow, where they were diligently studied at OKB-134. The opportunity to get acquainted with the weapon accelerated Soviet work on an identical class of AAMs.

It was quickly found that the American missile featured a number of technological innovations yet to be developed in the USSR that made it easier to mass-produce

OPPOSITE
The warhead in the nose section of the R-3S is clearly visible forward of the guidance vanes in this cross-sectioned example of the AAM. Weighting 11.3kg, the high-explosive "destroyer" warhead was filled with hexogen. When the missile either hit its target or the proximity fuze exploded, the body of the charge was torn into thousands of fragments that flew out in a cone shape from the nose of the AAM to a distance of about 20m, fatally damaging the target. (István Toperczer)

and operate. The simplicity of the AIM-9 contrasted with the complexity and poor quality of its Soviet counterparts. For example, the Sidewinder's infrared guidance system contained free gyroscopes of a much smaller size than those seen in Soviet AAMs, whilst its flight control system was incomparably better.

Armorers from the 921st FR attach an R-3S to the port APU-13 launch rail of MiG-21PFM "Red 5034" at Noi Bai. The R-3S, which could be launched at altitudes up to 21,000m, had an effective range of 8,000m. (István Toperczer Collection)

Gennadiy Sokolovskiy, who subsequently headed up the Vympel design bureau, stated, "The Sidewinder became a real 'university' for us, providing our engineers with a practical course in missile design that updated our approach to creating future AAMs."

The first test launches of the new K-13 (designated R-3 or Object 300 by the VVS) from a modified MiG-19 took place in March 1959, and it was cleared for mass production at several plants in February 1960. The missile, with a modified gas generator, became the K-13A (R-3S or Object 310) and entered service in 1962. It was approved for use by both the MiG-21F-13 and MiG-21PF. With the latter already overloaded by a third of a ton following airframe modifications to allow the installation of the RP-21 radar, the cannon armament seen in the F-13 had to be deleted to save weight.

VPAF MiG-21 pilots under training in the Soviet Union fired a number of R-3Ss at unmanned targets prior to completing their courses and returning to North Vietnam. As part of their tuition, they also had to learn how to use the RP-21 radar fitted in the "Fishbed-D/F." Nguyen Van Coc was amongst the pilots to receive training in the use of radar and missiles in the USSR:

> After the completion of the close attack syllabus, student pilots moved on to radar training and the employment of missiles for interception at long distances from low through to high altitude at both subsonic and supersonic speeds. Mastering the operation of the RP-21 radar at different altitudes and in various weather conditions was far from easy. When using radar only to detect a target, achieve the correct launch parameters, and fire the missile, the enemy aircraft would remain out of the pilot's sight. We had to practice such a scenario over and over again on the radar simulator at Krasnodar, students having to draw

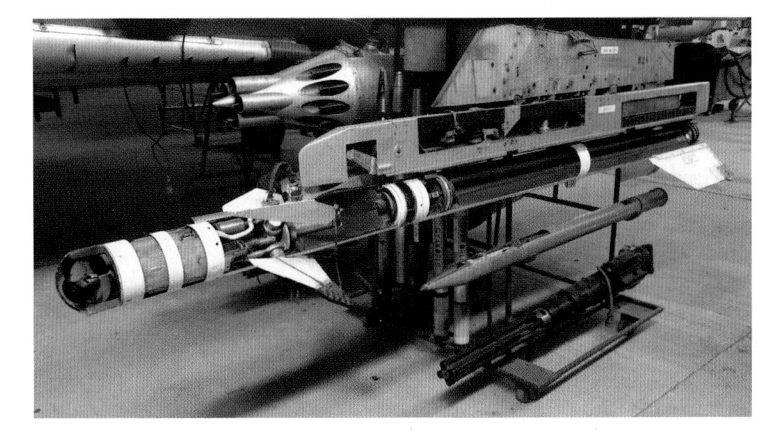

> on paper what was shown on a typical radar screen so that we could memorize various detection scenarios for employment when undertaking training missions.
>
> Having proved our familiarity with the basic functions of the RP-21, we were then sent to a firing range in Astrakhan Oblast to expend infrared and radar-guided AAMs. The range was in a desert in western USSR near where the Volga River met the Caspian Sea. Shortly after our arrival, we were schooled in the features of the local landscape, briefed on the flying rules, given the course timetable, told the types of weapon being fired, drilled on inflight communication, and shown what to do in an emergency.
>
> During the live-fire exercise with the R-3S, our target was a specially designed flaming oil tank hung beneath a parachute that had been dropped by a transport aircraft from an altitude of 8,000–10,000m. The burning tank created enough of a heat source for the missile to detect, the weapon self-adjusting its guidance vanes until the R-3S was within ten meters of the target, at which point its radio detonator would explode. Thousands of fragments then flew out in a cone shape from the nose of the AAM to a distance of about 20m, fatally damaging the target.

The RP-21 was used in the acquisition, tracking, and interception of aerial targets by day or night in all weathers, the radar having a continuously transmitting antenna that moved mechanically in horizontal lines +/-30 degrees from the centerline, as well as vertically +/-10 degrees. The antenna was gyro-stabilized between +/-60 degrees of bank and +/-40 degrees of pitch.

The radar's "real world" maximum detection range was just 13km, and it could lock on to a target up to seven kilometers away – but only from the rear hemisphere. Despite the RP-21 having improved protection against passive jamming, the interception of a target below 1,200m was impossible due to ground clutter. Its "dead range" was 900m or less because of the radar's relatively low frequency. The R-3S's narrow detection band and modest range meant that VPAF MiG-21 pilots relied almost exclusively on ground-based radar and GCI controllers for guidance when engaging enemy aircraft.

According to the VPAF, the first aerial victory credited to the MiG-21 was claimed with an R-3S by Nguyen Hong Nhi when he shot down a Firebee drone on March 4, 1966. The first successful interception of a manned aircraft came on September 21, 1966 after a strike force of F-105s and F-4s was detected passing over the Yen Tu mountains on its way to attack the Dap Cau road and railway bridge in Bac Giang Province, 24km northeast of Hanoi. The local command post ordered MiG-17s and MiG-21s to intercept the fighter-bombers, resulting in four "Fresco-Cs" being scrambled from Kien An at 0858 hrs. Ten minutes later, a

The RP-21 Sapfir ("Spin Scan") intercept radar fitted in the MiG-21PFL/PFM served as the aircraft's "all-seeing eyes" during aerial combat. Its primary task was to locate aircraft up to 15km away and to lock on to them from ten kilometers so as to allow the pilot to fire an AAM. The RP-21 could be operated in four different modes – search, acquisition, pursuit tracking, and fire control. (István Toperczer)

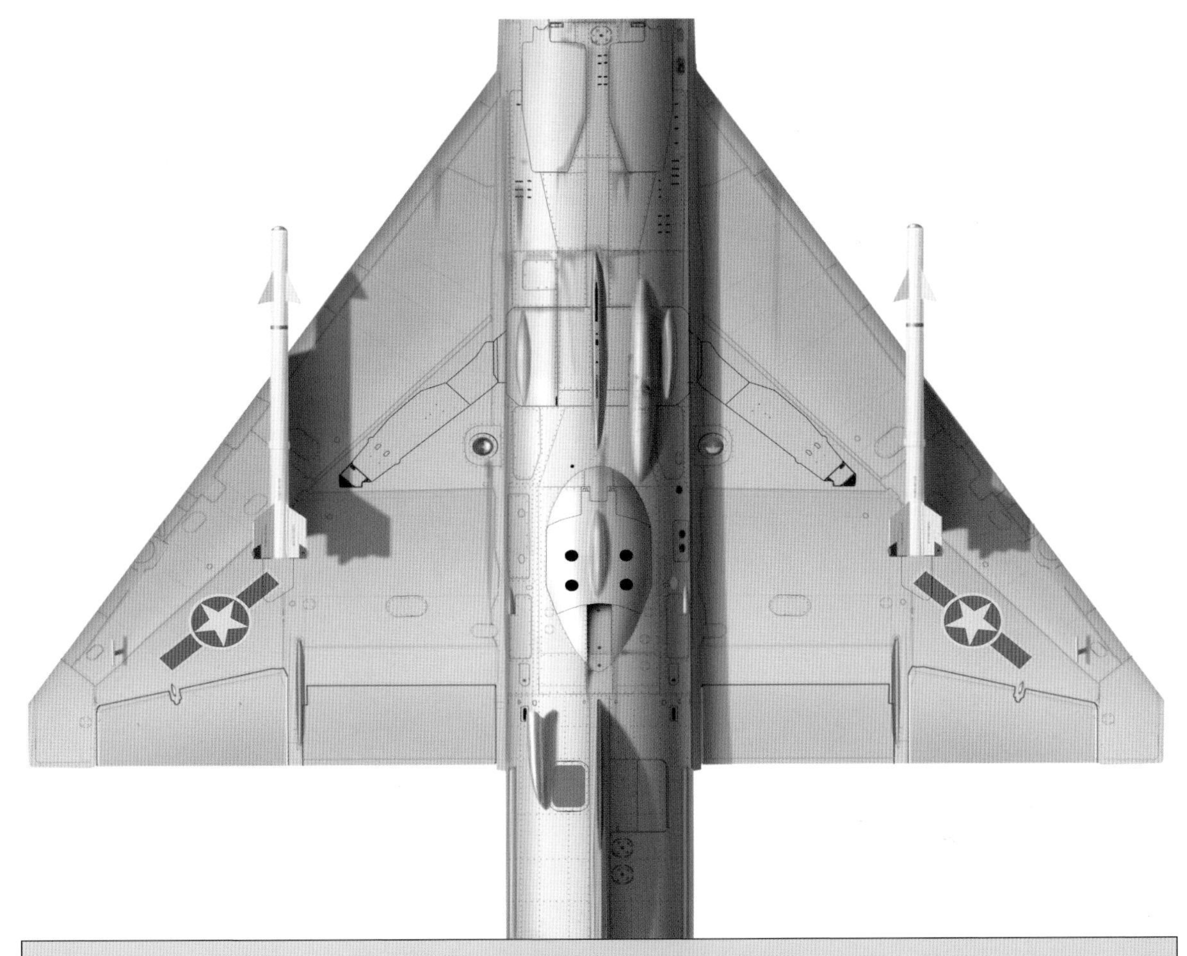

MiG-21PFL MISSILE ARMAMENT

The most effective weapon employed by VPAF MiG-21s during *Rolling Thunder* was the R-3S/K-13 (AA-2 "Atoll") infrared-homing AAM, a single example of which could be attached to an underwing APU-13M launcher. Weighing 75.3kg, the weapon boasted an 11.3kg high-explosive "destroyer" fragmentation warhead. The "Atoll", two of which were carried by the MiG-21F-13, MiG-21PFL, and MiG-21PFM, was essentially a copy of the American AIM-9B Sidewinder. The R-3S could be launched at altitudes up to 21,000m and had an effective range of 8,000m.

pair of MiG-21s flown by Le Trong Huyen and Tran Thien Luong departed Noi Bai and circled overhead their airfield, before being directed to a point 30km east of Luc Nam.

At 0920 hrs Huyen and Luong were able to exploit the F-4s' preoccupation with the MiG-17s to attack Thunderchiefs heading directly toward them. In the ensuing melee, Huyen downed F-105D 62-4371 (call-sign "Wildcat 1") flown by Capt G. L. Ammon of the 357th TFS/355th TFW with an R-3S, giving him the first of his four victories. Although the USAF claimed the jet had fallen victim to AAA northeast of Hanoi, in the wake of this engagement the Seventh Air Force alerted its units in-theater to the potency of the MiG-21 equipped with the R-3S AAM. The USAF was correct to do so, as Huyen had in fact fired his "Atoll" from a distance of 1,500m – the very limit of the targeting system's operational envelope – at a height of 1,200m and a speed of 700km/h.

The MiG-21PFL's canopy hinged at the front to open forward. The "Fishbed-D" used the same 62mm-thick bulletproof windshield as the earlier MiG-21F-13, and it also retained the smaller windows attached to either side of the windshield frame. The scope and rubber viewing hood for the RP-21 radar were mounted at the top of the instrument panel. The PKI-1 collimator gunsight was mounted above the radar scope and immediately aft of the bulletproof glass windshield. The PKI-1 allowed the pilot to visually aim his R-3S AAMs when the RP-21 was switched off. Controls for the radar and the ARK-10 Automatic Direction Finder were mounted on the right cockpit wall. (István Toperczer)

During early October three pairs of MiG-21s claimed three kills with "Atoll" missiles, but only the first of these victories, on the morning of the 5th, was acknowledged by the USAF as having fallen to the VPAF. That day, fighter-bomber formations were picked up on radar heading for the Moc Chau–Yen Bai area. Bui Dinh Kinh and Nguyen Danh Kinh (forming the attack flight), with Nguyen Nhat Chieu and Dang Ngoc Ngu in support, took off to intercept the enemy aircraft. After ten minutes the attack flight sighted four F-4Cs from the 433rd TFS/8th TFW 60km southwest of Yen Bai.

Assigned to escort two EB-66 Destroyer electronic warfare (EW) aircraft, the USAF fighters were circling at 30,000ft when they were surprised by the MiGs' attack. Bui Dinh Kinh fired his two R-3Ss and shot down Phantom II 64-0702 flown by 1Lt E. W. Garland (who subsequently reported that his jet had been hit by an 'Atoll') and Capt W. R. Andrews, the crew having been totally unaware of the MiGs' presence. This was the first time an F-4 had been downed by a MiG-21.

Kinh's success on 5 October not only convinced MiG-21 pilots of the soundness of their tactics and the effectiveness of the R-3S, it also showed VPAF Command and GCI personnel that the best way to direct and control "Fishbed" interceptions was to give pilots as much time as possible to get into a favorable attack position.

Cockpit

The forward fuselage of the MiG-21F-13 "Fishbed-C" and MiG-21PF "Fishbed-D" was assembled from four main sections. The third section, between bulkheads Nos. 6 and 11, contained the pressurized and airconditioned cockpit. It was constructed from bulkheads, longerons, and spars topped by a light alloy canopy frame. The latter, featuring an alcohol-based de-icing system, was opened with pressurized air. The windscreen was made from silicate glass with a total thickness of 14.5mm, while the rest of the canopy was glazed with 10mm acrylic glass. Inside the windscreen, a 62mm-thick bulletproof windshield was mounted immediately aft of the canopy hinge. The main canopy was hinged at the front to open forward.

Both the MiG-21F-13 and the MiG-21PFL were fitted with the Type SK (*Sistema Katapultirovaniya*) ejection seat, which could be safely used at speeds up to 1,100km/h and at altitudes above 110m. When the Type SK-1 ejection seat was activated, the pilot experienced a maximum force of 18G. The canopy was designed to protect him from the airflow when he left the cockpit, and it stayed with the seat during the initial phase of the ejection sequence.

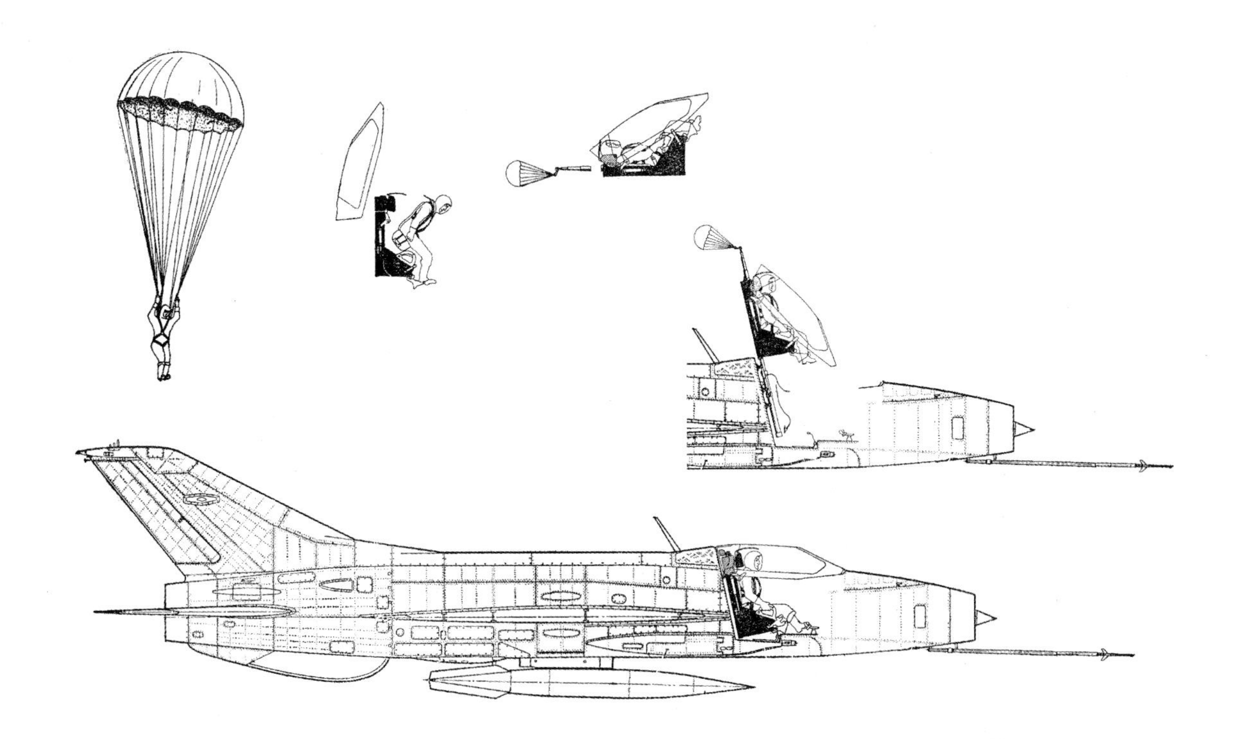

The phases of emergency ejection with the Type SK-1 seat from the MiG-21F-13 (which were exactly the same in the MiG-21PFL) are illustrated here in this diagram from the "Fishbed-C" manual. When the pilot pulled the activation handles to initiate ejection, the leg grippers pulled his lower limbs back towards the seat and his shoulder straps tightened. As the seat accelerated up the ejection rail, the main canopy was released from its fastening and it moved back to shelter the pilot from the slipstream. The stabilizer 'chute was also activated at this point. The pilot and the canopy descended to a safe altitude, at which point the stabilizer chute detached. The canopy fell away shortly thereafter and the straps and leg grippers unlocked, freeing the pilot from the seat. His main 'chute then deployed, and the pilot safely descended to the ground. (István Toperczer Collection)

Visibility from the cockpit of the MiG-21F-13 and MiG-21PFL was poor in all areas bar the forward quadrant above the horizon. The view through the gunsight and bulletproof glass was particularly restricted, and this seriously degraded visual target acquisition of aircraft the size of an F-4 Phantom II or F-105 Thunderchief. Indeed, pilots usually only spotted fighter-bombers through the front windscreen at a range of five to nine kilometers. The pilot's seating position and narrow canopy also caused severe visibility restrictions, with the view to the rear of the jet being limited to an area 50–60 degrees aft of the nose cone. Furthermore, the side-view in level flight was restricted to about 20 degrees below the horizon, and a metal flap attached to the ejection seat above the pilot's head restricted upper visibility.

MiG-21 pilots flying in pairs did not depend on mutual support from each other when attacking aircraft from behind, as this task was assigned to the GCI controller. This meant that no "Fishbeds" could attack targets beyond the range of GCI radar coverage, despite the fact that MiG-21s fitted with external fuel tanks (as VPAF examples almost always were) exceeded the range of the ground-based radar.

The MiG-21PFM "Fishbed-F" that directly followed the MiG-21PFL "Fishbed-D" was fitted with a more conventional fixed windscreen and sideways-opening canopy. The jet's armored windscreen featured three separate sheets of silicate glass with a combined thickness of 14.5mm, while the port and starboard windshield panes and canopy again featured 10mm acrylic glass. The hinged main canopy opened to the starboard side, and it was supported by a foldable strut when open. The MiG-21PFM was the first variant equipped with mirrors on the canopy frame to improve the pilot's rearward visibility.

An early version of the KM-1 (SK-3) ejection seat replaced the Type SK-1 in the MiG-21PFM, its rails and locks being hinged to the cockpit floor. The new system enabled safe ejections from zero altitude up to 25,000m, with a minimum speed of 130km/h during a take-off run/landing roll and a maximum speed of 1,200km/h. The pilot was automatically separated from his seat at a safe distance (45m) from the aircraft, although a manual separation arm could be used if the automatic device failed.

Between 1966–68 many VPAF MiG-21 pilots were forced to eject during aerial battles, with several surviving multiple ejections in a short period of time. Nguyen Dang Kinh, Dong Van Song, and Vu Ngoc Dinh ejected three times in combat within a year, while Nguyen Hong Nhi, Bui Duc Nhu, and Mai Van Cuong ejected twice. Vu Dinh Rang was also shot down twice in just four days, successfully ejecting on both occasions. According to Vu Ngoc Dinh:

> Following an ejection, we were given a thorough examination in a military hospital. If no injuries were found and we were not complaining of aches and pains after the event, we were usually assigned combat alert duty once again within a few days. It was total war, and every pilot was needed for there were never many of us. I ejected on January 2, 1967 during Operation *Bolo* [when World War II ace Col Robin Olds led the F-4C-equipped 8th TFW in an operation to neutralize the 921st FR]. Four months later, on May 20, my MiG-21 was hit and I had to eject again. This time I lost consciousness for a few seconds, and I eventually came to my senses when hanging beneath my parachute. The cords of my 'chute were tangled, but I managed to free them and land safely. With no injuries and no complaints, I was back on duty 48 hours later.
>
> According to the general procedure observed by the VPAF, if we suffered any health problems following an ejection, we were grounded from one to three months depending on the severity of the issue.

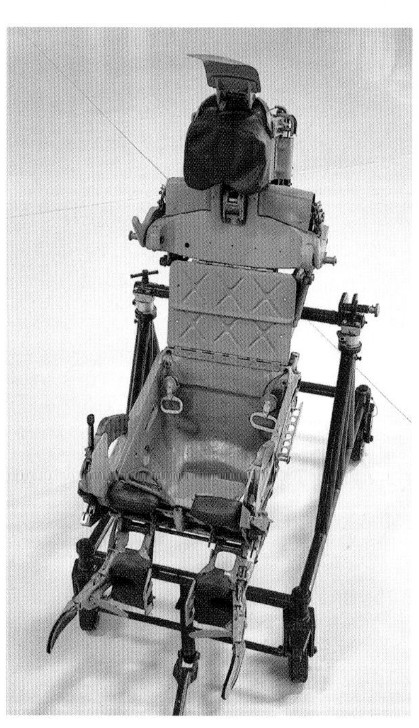

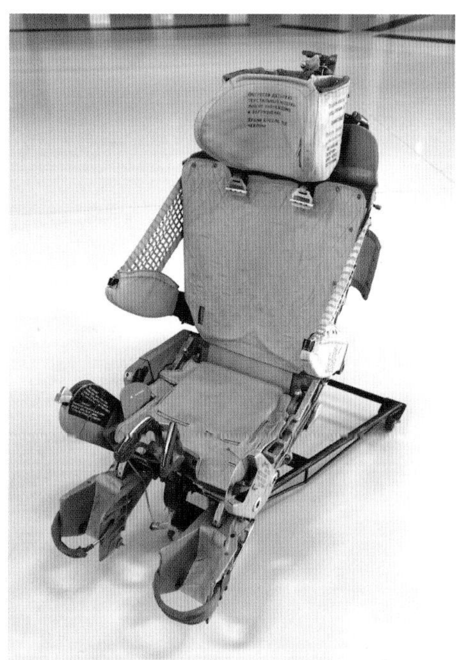

RIGHT
Both the MiG-21F-13 and the MiG-21PFL were fitted with the Type SK-1 ejection seat, which could only be safely used at speeds up to 1,100km/h and at altitudes above 110m. By pulling one of the red handles (on either side of the seat near the pilot's thighs or between his legs), a PK-3M-1 pyrotechnic cartridge was activated that ignited the TSM-2500-38 solid rocket motor. The SK-1 was equipped with an AD-3U computer timer and a KAP-3 separation device which combined to ensure that the pilot and seat separated 1.5 seconds after ejection. (István Toperczer)

FAR RIGHT
The MiG-21PFM was equipped with the more advanced KM-1 (SK-3) ejection seat. A stabilizing parachute was mounted inside the headrest that combined with a PZ-1 rocket motor to pull the seat clear of the aircraft. The pilot was separated from the KM-1 by a pre-set automatic device, or by a manual separation arm if the latter failed to operate. The KM-1 allowed safe ejections at speeds ranging from 130km/h to 1,200km/h and up to an altitude of 25,000m. (István Toperczer)

CHAPTER 5
ART OF WAR

As previously explained in this volume, North Vietnamese MiG pilots and senior staff officers received their initial military and flight training in the USSR, so the formations, tactics, and force employment philosophy of the VPAF duly evolved from Soviet doctrine. Flight formations developed by VVS instructors were, for example, devised for defense and attack in a GCI-friendly operational environment.

Prior to and during World War II, the VVS's primary task was to control the skies immediately overhead Red Army troops on the frontline. However, with the development in the West of strategic jet bombers capable of carrying nuclear weapons, the VVS began to field supersonic aircraft armed with AAMs which, in conjunction with ground-based SAMs and more effective long-range radar, undertook the air defense of the USSR.

VVS units charged with protecting the Soviet Union honed their "interception" skills throughout the 1950s, pilots being vigorously trained in how to effectively intercept enemy aircraft en route to their targets. They were taught how best to use the high speed of their interceptors to engage bombers while they were still inbound, with the primary purpose of such an attack being to break up the formation and repel the enemy before their own fighter escorts could protect them.

Following the VVS lead, the VPAF's definition of "interception" stated that it was "a method of preparation and practice of aerial combat with fighters, supported by other air defense forces, aimed at breaking down enemy formations and destroying their bombers on their intended route to their target."

According to the VVS tactical doctrine taught to VPAF MiG-21 pilots, "aerial combat" was a series of offensive maneuvers that ended with a successful weapon launch to defeat the enemy. The approach phase of aerial combat would see the pilot maneuver his jet to allow him to identify his target either visually or via radar, before closing in on the enemy aircraft so as to get into an advantageous position for an attack. This engagement phase was of critical importance in aerial combat, as it was when the fighter pilot had to destroy his target.

Two combat alert MiG-21PFMs overfly Noi Bai in a "pair patrol" tactical formation after being scrambled in 1968. The wingman is echeloned 20–30 degrees behind his leader. Both "Fishbed-Fs" are armed with two R-3S AAMs, and lack centerline drop tanks. The absence of the latter indicates that the pilots have been sent aloft on a local airfield defense mission. (István Toperczer Collection)

His attack maneuver started with him aiming his jet at his opponent in order to achieve a radar lock-on, after which he fired his AAM. Continuous maneuvering during the attack would be followed by a quick break-off from the pursuit of the target in order to reduce the possibility of being hit by hostile defensive fire. It also allowed the pilot to assume an advantageous position for a follow-on attack or the interception of another target aircraft.

VVS instructors went to great pains to teach their students about the rules that had to be followed during aerial combat. They were told to avoid flying in cloud cover; never fly closer to a target than the prescribed weapon engagement distance; do not descend below 2,000m; do not attack into the sun; avoid flying into the target's exhaust efflux; and maintain continuous visual contact with the enemy.

Slightly different maneuvers and techniques would be used if more than one MiG-21 pilot was involved in the interception. Again, attacks by two or more "Fishbeds" were to be executed sequentially. An attack executed by a single interceptor armed with two AAMs was to be undertaken from behind, above, from either side, or through a combination of all of these directions. Simultaneous attacks by multiple MiG-21s could be executed from various directions against enemy aircraft – or helicopters – flying in formation. During an attack, each pilot independently aimed and launched his missile against a single target.

VPAF students were taught that the aerial combat sequence detailed earlier in this chapter could be performed by a single aircraft or a pair or quartet of fighters. When multiple MiG-21s were involved, pilots flew in loose line astern formation with gaps between jets that allowed for an immediate AAM launch without the possibility of downing a friendly fighter. The lead pilot would immediately break off his attack once his missile had been launched, giving his wingman a clear view of additional targets and an unobstructed firing path for his weapon.

In Soviet flying schools, offensive ("Angle," "Roll," "Hook," "Fork" and "Roof") and defensive ("Knot," "Shell," "Loop" and "Crab") maneuvers were taught which took into account the azimuth angle and altitude of the enemy aircraft, and determined the position of the MiG-21s in their own two- or four-ship formations. The "Snake" maneuver, which was popular with "Fishbed" pilots, had both defensive ("Knot") and offensive ("Roof") elements to it.

Initially, the VPAF fielded mixed formations of MiG-17s and MiG-21s during early operations with the "Fishbed" in 1966. The "Fresco" pilots would be tasked with engaging enemy aircraft at low altitude (up to 1,500m), while the MiG-21s patroled at higher ceilings (in excess of 2,500m). The airspace between 1,500–2,500m was considered to be an "intermediate zone" in which both aircraft types could operate in case an interception evolved into a dogfight.

MiG-21 "SNAKE" MANEUVER

This diagram shows the complex "Snake" maneuver employed by two pairs of MiG-21s ("Red") after they had been targeted by a two-ship of USAF F-4 Phantom IIs ("Blue"):
1 – Two MiG-21 pairs ("Red 01" leading and "Red 02" trailing) are flying 2.5–3km apart in line abreast, with each pair in loose echelon 600–800m apart and with the wingmen at an angle of 20 degrees off the tail of their respective leaders.
2 – An F-4 two-ship attacks "Red 01."
3 – The lead MiG-21 pilot of "Red 01" performs a defensive "Knot" maneuver, which consists of a right half-loop, in response to being attacked.
4 – "Red 01's" wingman, meanwhile, banks into a tight level turn to the right.
5 – The F-4 pair also split formation, with the leader pursuing the "Red 01" lead.
6 – The F-4 wingman attacks his opposite number in the "Red 01" formation, pursuing in a level turn.
7 – Meanwhile, the "Red 02" pair perform a "Roof" maneuver.
8 – "Red 02" lead attacks the lead F-4 from behind after flying a half-loop.
9 – "Red 02's" wingman engages the Phantom II wingman following a level turn that places him directly behind the USAF fighter.

Combat alert duty pilots Vu Ngoc Dinh and Dong Van Song run to their MiG-21PFLs at Noi Bai in early 1966. Behind R-3S-armed "Red 4324" is a covered earth shelter for technical equipment used in the servicing of "Fishbeds" at the airfield. "Red 4324" would subsequently enjoy success in aerial combat with no fewer than nine pilots – Le Trong Huyen, Pham Thanh Ngan, Nguyen Ngoc Do, Nguyen Van Ly, Nguyen Hong Nhi, Dang Ngoc Ngu, Nguyen Van Coc, Vu Ngoc Dinh, and Nguyen Dang Kinh – during 1967. (István Toperczer Collection)

Between April–September 1966, MiG-21s had participated in a number of aerial battles that had seen pilots given GCI guidance according to the "traditional interception" methods espoused by the VVS. On every occasion the "Fishbed" pilots had run into trouble with USAF and US Navy fighters, resulting in them enjoying little in the way of success and suffering a number of losses.

Because of the interception techniques being used and the AAMs employed (predominantly "Alkali" semi-active radar-homing weapons), pilots had been instructed by GCI to focus on their radar screens and fly straight and level for extended periods as they were guided in behind enemy aircraft. With the MiG-21's forward vision from the cockpit being notoriously bad, it was difficult to visually acquire the target when the fighter's radar failed to detect it or the enemy used a jamming device to block the system.

Furthermore, activation of the RP-21 alerted enemy aircraft to the MiG-21's presence due to the fitment of radar warning receivers (RWRs) in all US combat aircraft. Once such a threat had been detected, enemy pilots usually commenced violent evasive maneuvers aimed at preventing their opponents from achieving a missile lock. Such flying was usually enough to defeat the RP-21 and break the radar lock for the G-limited "Alkali."

First Manned Combat

The first MiG-21 combat with a manned opponent came on April 23, 1966, when Nguyen Dang Kinh and Dong Van Song attacked a flight of F-105s and their F-4 escorts. However, they were unable to fire their R-3Ss and S-5Ms as they failed to achieve the correct launch parameters. The hydraulic system on Kinh's "Red 4121" was damaged during the action and he was forced to eject from an altitude of 200m – he landed safely in the village of Ninh Giang, in Kim Anh District. According to USAF records, two F-4C crews (from the 555th TFS/8th TFW) each claimed a MiG-17 kill that day. There was no mention of any MiG-21s being engaged.

Three days later, Nguyen Hong Nhi and Dong Van Song took off from Noi Bai in an attempt to intercept an EB-66 EW aircraft – a highly sought after target for all VPAF pilots. The Destroyer's F-4C escorts from the 480th TFS/35th TFW intervened over Bac Can, near Thai Nguyen, and the combat ended badly for the VPAF when Maj P. J. Gilmore and 1Lt W. T. Smith used a Sidewinder to claim the first MiG-21 credited to a US aircraft. Nhi was the unlucky pilot, being forced to eject from "Red 4028":

> That day, the American pilots saw our MiG-21s and attacked us in order to defend the EB-66 they were protecting. We had spotted two F-4s escorting the EW aircraft,

and I decided to pursue the fighter to the left. They accelerated and made good their escape. Just as I was about to pull up to gain altitude, a streak of light flashed past my cockpit – an AAM had been fired at me but it had just missed. I immediately looked to my rear and to either side, and it was only then that I saw multiple F-4s all around me. I was trapped in the middle of a formation of enemy fighters.

As I pulled my MiG into a tight banking turn, with the intention of chasing one of the F-4s, I felt my aircraft shudder slightly – it had been hit by a Sidewinder. I leveled out and pushed the throttle forward to maximum power in an attempt to make it back to Noi Bai. However, my aircraft began to lose speed and altitude and the hydraulic system's low pressure warning light came on. When my altitude was down to 3,000m and I realized that I could no longer control my MiG, I decided to eject. I suffered a serious spinal injury upon landing, and had to undergo medical treatment for an extended period of time.

On March 4, 1966, future ace Nguyen Hong Nhi used an R-3S to shoot down a Firebee drone at high altitude north of Hanoi to record the first aerial victory by a MiG-21 over North Vietnam. He was in turn shot down on 26 April by an F-4C from the 480th TFS/35th TFW, his MiG-21PFL "Red 4028" being hit by a Sidewinder northeast of Hanoi. Nhi would survive three ejections during *Rolling Thunder*. (István Toperczer Collection)

Shortly thereafter, during a conference called by VPAF Command and the 921st FR, it was pointed out that even though the unit had been well-prepared and had flown numerous combat missions, its efficiency was low and, moreover, an aircraft had been lost. Pilots presented detailed briefings on every phase of the battles they had been involved in, together with their assessments of the enemy's tactics. During these discussions the pilots said the primary reason for the MiG-21's lack of success was that its capabilities had not been fully exploited. Indeed, a suitable attack procedure for the Mach 2.0-capable interceptor had yet to be devised.

Analysis of dogfights in April–May 1966 had shown that for pilots the most difficult part of an engagement was keeping a rapidly moving target centered within their gunsights. The MiG-21's optical sighting system was used for target acquisition, with radar targeting employed only for search and rangefinding, or when using an "Alkali" AAM. This meant that the pilot had to judge the range before adopting the optimal launch position and reaching the weapon engagement zone. The ability to judge distance had still to be learned.

Furthermore, some pilots continued to employ MiG-17 combat tactics, attempting to enter turning dogfights in their much-faster but less agile MiG-21s. In short, they were not yet proficient in using their aircraft's weapons – proving this point, no fewer than 14 R-3Ss and a handful of RS-2USs had been fired during three engagements in April–May 1966 and not one had hit its target.

Faced with such a poor performance, VPAF Command suspended "Fishbed" combat operations while the training of new tactics was hastily arranged. The latter included revised command and GCI procedures that defined optimum takeoff times, selected correct attack positions, and judged the right attack speed and range for successful missile firing. Despite time being needed to allow pilots (including 13 new arrivals who returned to North Vietnam from the USSR in June) to implement these changes, the increasing tempo of US air strikes precluded this.

During the mission hiatus, the 921st FR worked hard at determining the optimum time needed to successfully scramble MiG-21s in order for pilots to make a curving approach from a higher altitude behind target aircraft so that they could visually spot enemy jets at the earliest possible opportunity. Intercepting pilots would then have a tactical advantage in respect to speed and altitude when choosing the optimum approach angle for an attack.

The tactics used by the 921st FR steadily evolved during the course of *Rolling Thunder*. Initially, pilots rigidly stuck to what they had been taught about effective interception by their VVS instructors. When this proved less than successful, they studied the air combat methods employed by MiG-17 pilots. The often unique local weather conditions were also taken into account, as were the tactics used by their enemy. Finally, all of these factors, combined with the growing operational experience of the "Fishbed" pilots themselves, saw the 921st settle on a series of more suitable interception methods that turned the MiG-21 into an effective fighter in the skies over North Vietnam.

The unit's primary task remained the interception of enemy fighter-bombers attempting to attack targets, and VPAF Command, GCI officers posts, and the pilots themselves changed a number of guidance methods in order to give them a tactical advantage when engaging aircraft in combat situations. The emergence of new tactics that were more flexible in their execution took the enemy by surprise.

The most important factor in a successful interception was spotting the hostile aircraft from as great a distance as possible. Achieving this 300–400km from the target area was all but impossible, for the VPAF lacked sufficient intelligence resources (forward observers, ground-based radar, etc.). This in turn meant that MiG-21 pilots were often scrambled too late, resulting in them clashing with fighter-bombers, and their escorts, as they neared the target area. Forced into hasty, turning, pursuits, "Fishbed" pilots had to launch their AAMs in sub-optimal conditions and rarely enjoyed any success. Eventually, a ground-based radar system that was capable of detecting enemy aircraft at distances of up to 250km was deployed near the Vietnamese–Laotian border. This greatly increased the chances of MiG-21 pilots being scrambled well in advance of approaching enemy formations.

Having understood that classical VVS interception techniques were not entirely suited to operations over North Vietnam, the VPAF also concluded that a "Fishbed" could not be flown like a "Fresco" in aerial combat. The mind-set of senior commanders and pilots had to change accordingly, as did GCI techniques when it came to guiding MiG-21 flights into successful positions from which to engage the enemy.

Such interception missions had to be undertaken in accordance with the reality of the conflict in North Vietnam, rather than the European battlefield for which the MiG-21 had been designed. The "Fishbed" had been created for the interception of NATO bombers and ground-attack aircraft, with the fighter almost always approaching the target from behind at a distance of 8–12km

MiG-21 TACTICAL FORMATIONS

The VPAF's original two-ship formation (leader and wingman – top) and subsequent four-ship formation (bottom) was at the heart of all aerial combat tactics employed by MiG-21 pilots during *Rolling Thunder*. Once in the air, a two-ship formation of "Fishbeds" was separated by 50–200m, while each of the pairs in a four-ship formation flew 300–700m apart. These distances were subsequently changed to 500–800m for a two-ship formation and 800–1,500m for two pairs in a four-ship.

MiG-21 pilots in two- or four-ship formations could only operate independently of one another after they had climbed to an altitude in excess of 2,500m. The leader was the attacker, while his wingman was tasked with watching their rear hemisphere when intercepting American aircraft. They had the flexibility to change positions, and roles, should the aerial situation require the wingman to become the "shooter." VPAF pilots often targeted the No. 4 jet in American four-ship formations, as this aircraft was particularly vulnerable to attacks from the rear.

under the direction of GCI. Although the jet's RP-21 was capable of detecting a target at a range of 7–13km, the effective launch distance of both its R-3S and RS-2US AAMs was only about 1–3km.

During a "traditional" interception, when MiG-21 pilots were using their RP-21 radars and had to rigidly follow the enemy from behind along a longitudinal axis, they were unable to observe other groups of American aircraft in the immediate vicinity, making them easy targets for enemy fighters. The latter were usually armed with AIM-9B Sidewinders, which were particularly effective against MiG-21s flying straight and level for an extended period of time during a "traditional" interception.

When "Fishbed" pilots attacked in pairs, it was the job of the wingman to watch the rear hemisphere for approaching enemy fighters and/or AAMs. When he saw a missile launch, he would immediately yell out a warning over the radio so that both he and his leader could perform high-G turns into and below the weapon. This maneuver would usually break the lock of the AIM-9's infrared seeker head on the MiG-21's tailpipe. Violent maneuvering was also used to defeat the AIM-7E Sparrow III semi-active radar homing AAM used exclusively by the Phantom II.

The MiG-21's principle targets during *Rolling Thunder* were F-4s and F-105s, and both jets were equipped with RWRs that identified whether it was ground guidance radar or aircraft target acquisition radar that had detected them. This proved particularly problematic for MiG-21 pilots, whose presence had already been detected despite their aircraft being well short of reaching the launch zone for an AAM. With the element of surprise well and truly lost, and their target aircraft maneuvering to avoid interception, VPAF pilots were forced to either engage in aerial combat or break off and return to base.

As previously noted in this chapter, for the MiG-21 to achieve optimal performance against incoming fighter-bomber formations targeting North Vietnam, enemy aircraft had to be detected at a distance of 150–200km so that the 921st FR could get jets in the air and GCI could coordinate an effective long-range interception. However, Vietnam is a narrow country geographically, and it was therefore impossible to apply traditional GCI methods to protect targets, as was the case in larger countries.

In the east, for example, the distance from the coast to targets in North Vietnam was very short, allowing US Navy strike groups flying from carriers on *Yankee Station* (just 90 miles offshore in the Gulf of Tonkin) a quick approach to their targets. Although the distance from their bases in Thailand to the North Vietnamese border was relatively long for USAF fighter-bombers, the actual time they spent in communist airspace heading for targets was again quite short – 10–15 minutes at the speeds typically flown by Phantom IIs and Thunderchiefs. US strike packages continuously changed the routes they used when ingressing to targets so as to make it harder for MiG-21s to undertake successful rear hemisphere attacks.

It was, therefore, extremely difficult for GCI personnel to determine exactly when to order jets aloft to intercept enemy aircraft. For such a decision to be made with any confidence, they needed up-to-date strategic intelligence from border-based radar sites and guidance systems, a sound working knowledge of previous mission profiles undertaken by the USAF and US Navy, and a thorough understanding of the enemy's seasonal operational profile over North Vietnam.

With all of this taken into consideration, the role of the MiG-21 during *Rolling Thunder* evolved as better tactics were used by the VPAF. From April 1966 to January 1967, "Fishbed" pilots initially studied how best to fight American aircraft. VPAF Command was wary of its GCI vectoring MiG-21s in the direction of enemy fighter-bombers at greater distances and then being unable to effectively control the ensuing interception because it lacked a sufficiently detailed radar picture to alert pilots about exactly how many jets they were engaging.

As already noted, during early operations, the lack of strategic intelligence caused by the paucity of radar systems in North Vietnam usually prevented GCI from ordering MiG-21s aloft at the right time to ensure an advantageous interception. This meant that "Fishbed" pilots often engaged enemy aircraft immediately after they had bombed their targets and were heading home. In an effort to score a victory before the jets fled the area, pilots took on their opponents in turning dogfights that usually ended without success.

In the summer of 1966, US strike packages commenced attacks on targets in Hanoi, Haiphong and in other military and industrial centers. From early July of that year, MiG-21s again started to undertake combat alert duty, with pilots now ready to use their new tactics against an increasingly powerful enemy. The 921st FR orchestrated some early engagements to test out the new tactics, with MiG-21s intercepting enemy aircraft in the immediate vicinity of Noi Bai. "Fishbeds" would now also launch coordinated attacks with "Fresco-Cs," both types undertaking combat air patrols (CAPs) along the main approach routes for US fighter-bombers heading for the Hanoi area.

Target Selection

Toward the end of the summer it became clear that MiG pilots were avoiding combat with USAF F-4s wherever possible. Indeed, VPAF Command's unofficial policy seemed to be that whenever the victory–loss ratio favored the enemy, fighter regiments were instructed not to engage in combat and prioritize the evaluation and revision of their tactics instead.

From mid-September onward, MiG-21s tentatively appeared once again, with their pilots having been told to focus on downing the more vulnerable F-105. As part of this strategy, the "Fishbeds" would undertake most of the high-altitude interception tasking, whilst the MiG-17s stuck to engaging enemy aircraft at lower altitudes.

September 1966 also saw the introduction of electronic countermeasures (ECM) pods under the wings of American fighter-bombers, as both the USAF and US Navy tried to defeat North Vietnamese radar (ground-based and the MiG-21's RP-21). Again, VPAF fighter activity dropped off, with US intelligence stating that MiG engagements had decreased by two-thirds.

Fully aware of the threat posed by the enemy's EW support aircraft in-theater, and now faced with increased ECM thanks to the fielding of the new pods by F-4s and F-105s, the 921st FR was instructed to renew its efforts to down an EB-66 in an effort to boost morale within the VPAF. MiG-21 pilots came close

Dong Van Song, who would be credited with four victories, was shot down by a 480th TFS/ 366th TFW F-4C near Hanoi on November 5, 1966 after he became target fixated with another Phantom II and failed to spot the danger behind him. (István Toperczer Collection)

on October 5, when Bui Dinh Kinh succeeding in destroying an escorting F-4C – this was the first time the USAF acknowledged the loss of a Phantom II to an R-3S.

An engagement on November 5 also saw "Fishbed" pilots clash with Destroyer escorts, and come close to downing an EB-66. The latter was being used to jam North Vietnamese search radar in an attempt to shield approaching fighter-bombers heading for targets in RP-6 north of Hanoi, four F-4Cs protecting the lone Destroyer as it flew an oval "racetrack" pattern near the target area.

At 1430 hrs Bui Dinh Kinh and Dong Van Song took off from Noi Bai and sighted the EW aircraft and its escorts at a range of ten kilometers. Ignoring the Phantom IIs, Kinh fired an R-3S at the EB-66 but missed when the pilot of the latter machine threw his aircraft into a diving spiral. The Destroyer then disappeared into cloud cover at an altitude of 3,000m, and when it emerged Kinh turned toward the aircraft in order carry to out a follow-up attack. His MiG-21 then became virtually uncontrollable, and Kinh realized that "Red 4022" had been hit by a missile. He quickly ejected. His assailant had been the F-4C of Maj J. E. Tuck and 1Lt J. J. Rabeni of the 480th TFS/366th TFW, the crew having used an AIM-7E Sparrow to down the MiG-21. They had in turn been targeted by Song, who, having maneuvered in behind the Phantom II, was just about to fire an R-3S when his 'Red 4026' was also hit by a missile (an AIM-9B) fired from the F-4C of 1Lts W. J. Latham and K. J. Klause. He too ejected and landed safely.

During the post-engagement debriefing the MiG-21 pilots admitted they had been too eager to attack the EB-66, and had not kept a close enough watch on the F-4s behind them. The cooperation between the two pilots had been inadequate, and Kinh had not looked behind him properly prior to firing his missile and commencing a break-away maneuver.

Between December 2–24, American jets flew 280 bombing missions over North Vietnam, their main targets being in the Hanoi area. They included the Yen Vien, Van Dien, and Gia Lam railway marshaling yards and Noi Bai and Kep airfields. The VPAF had little option but to commit aircraft in the defense of the capital. Initially, "Fishbeds" had operated in pairs during the type's early months in service. However, from October 5, 1966 through to January 6, 1967, in response to the escalating offensive against Hanoi, they sortied in four-ship formations on 12 occasions in an effort to blunt the strikes.

MiG-21 pilots participated in eight aerial battles during December, and claimed to have shot down nine USAF aircraft. The first clash, on the 2nd, took place when Noi Bai's fuel farm was attacked by F-105s, which also had an F-4 escort. Two MiG-21 pairs, comprising Vu Ngoc Dinh and Nghiem Dinh Hieu and Le Trong Huyen and Tran Thien Luong, were scrambled. Dinh subsequently recalled:

> I ordered the other pilots to drop their auxiliary fuel tanks and to accelerate as we attacked. I had split the four-ship formation into two sections and, turning inside the enemy aircraft, I managed to get in behind the F-105s. My wingman

BOTTOM
Future ace Vu Ngoc Dinh claimed his first aerial victory on December 5, 1966, and another kill followed exactly two weeks later. According to VPAF records, his victims on both occasions were F-105 Thunderchiefs, although neither claim was corroborated by USAF loss records. Dinh had trained to fly the MiG-17 between 1962–64, before converting to the MiG-21 in the USSR in 1965–66. His service with the 921st FR began in 1964, and VPAF records credit him with six aerial victories (five F-105s and an HH-53B helicopter) during the war. (István Toperczer Collection)

fired a missile at one, but the range was too great and it missed. Meanwhile, Huyen was chasing another. After one complete circle in a turning dogfight, he fired an R-3S at a Thunderchief from a range of 1,200m, scoring a kill. His wingman, Luong, wasn't able to fire his UB rocket pods because the range was too great.

On September 21, 1966, Le Trong Huyen claimed his first aerial victory when he shot down the 357th TFS/355th TFW F-105D of Capt G. L. Ammon near Bac Ninh, although the USAF attributed the loss to AAA. (István Toperczer Collection)

The USAF claimed that Capt M. L. Moorberg's F-105D (from the 34th TFS/388th TFW) had been shot down by 37mm AAA fire. Two F-4Cs from the 366th TFW's 480th and 389th TFSs were also destroyed during the Noi Bai attack, these being claimed by the 921st FR but credited to SAMs by the USAF.

On December 4, four MiG-21 pairs (comprising Dong Van De, Nguyen Van Coc, Nguyen Ngoc Do and Pham Thanh Ngan and Tran Ngoc Siu, Mai Van Cuong, Hoang Bieu and Dang Ngoc Ngu) were on combat alert duty at Noi Bai. Each flight leader's aircraft was armed with R-3Ss, while the wingmen's jets were equipped with rocket pods – the MiG-21s assigned to Bieu and Ngu had R-3Ss, however. They engaged USAF aircraft over Noi Bai, firing a total of five AAMs and 64 rockets. Although no enemy aircraft were shot down, the USAF crews were forced to jettison their bombs prior to reaching their target in order to make good their escape.

Up until this particular interception, the tactics employed by the 921st FR had seen its pilots remain in the vicinity of Noi Bai and commit to intercepts only when American aircraft intruded into their particular airspace. However, Soviet advisors had recommended that engagement areas be moved away from the intended target, which in turn meant that a US strike package would still be in close formation when VPAF fighters found it.

This happened again on December 5, when three pairs of MiG-21s were scrambled from Noi Bai after a 24-strong formation of F-105s was detected approaching from Thailand. At 0855 hrs Nguyen Dang Kinh and Bui Duc Nhu took off and were told to fly a holding pattern over Son Duong, some 35km away, and await the arrival of the Thunderchiefs. After flying one complete circle at an altitude of 3,000m, they sighted the F-105s in extended trail formation. At 0902 hrs Kinh attacked the lead flight, firing an R-3S that hit 62-4331 flown by Maj B. N. Begley. The USAF claimed that the F-105D, from the 421st TFS/388th TFW, had been shot down by a MiG-17.

That same afternoon another group of F-105s was detected over North Vietnam. Two MiG-21 pairs, comprising Le Trong Huyen and Tran Thien Luong and Vu Ngoc Dinh and Nghiem Dinh Hieu, took off and were directed to intercept over the Vinh Yen–Dai Tu–Doan Hung area. Vu Ngoc Dinh recalled the subsequent engagement:

We were flying along the Tam Dao mountains when I saw four black spots flying past 90 degrees off my nose. I immediately reported them

After each aerial engagement, the pilots involved discussed the experiences of the dogfight amongst themselves in informal debriefings such as this one staged for the camera in front of "Red 4225." Squatting at far left, future ace Nguyen Nhat Chieu explains details of an inconclusive action he fought in December 1966 to, from left to right, Dong Van De, Pham Thanh Ngan, Hoang Bieu, Mai Van Cuong, and Dang Ngoc Ngu. (István Toperczer Collection)

to the command post, which ordered us to attack. I got on an F-105's tail and tried to get closer, but when I could not do so I pulled up and went after another F-105. I chased it and fired my missile at it. I saw the missile hit the jet's tail, leaving the F-105 trailing smoke. We returned and landed safely. It was my first victory, and at that point I had only 23 flying hours as a second lieutenant on MiG-21s.

USAF records did not confirm this loss, however.

On December 14, eight MiG-21s in two flights, comprising Nguyen Nhat Chieu, Dang Ngoc Ngu, Dong Van De and Nguyen Van Coc and Pham Thanh Ngan, Hoang Bieu, Tran Ngoc Siu, and Mai Van Cuong, were on combat alert duty at Noi Bai. As with all MiG-21 flights, the second and fourth aircraft were equipped with rocket pods. The first flight took off at 1455 hrs, before being directed to a holding area over the Hoa Binh–Van Yen area. After making three complete circuits over the area, the "Fishbed" pilots spotted 20 F-105s flying near the northern slopes of the Tam Dao mountains, heading for Hanoi. The MiG-21s attacked.

Covered by Chieu, Ngu got on the tail of an F-105, forcing the attackers to drop their bombs in order to accelerate and turn away. Chieu and Ngu continued the pursuit until the GCI command post ordered the MiG pilots to turn back. Two more F-105 flights were then detected, and Chieu was chasing one when Ngu told him to turn sharply. Chieu banked violently to the right and an F-105 flashed past the upturned belly of his aircraft. He gave chase and fired an R-3S, but it failed to guide. Meanwhile, future ace Ngu shot down an F-105, although its loss was not confirmed by USAF sources.

While Chieu and Ngu were busy with their F-105s, De and Coc, whose jet was armed with rocket pods, turned to pursue a fourth Thunderchief flight. Coc later recalled:

> The F-105s discovered that we were behind them so they dropped their bombs and turned to escape. In accordance with our orders, we did not chase them very far before turning back in the direction of Noi Bai. Whilst returning, we spotted four more enemy aircraft in front of us. My leader got on the tail of an F-105 and fired his missile, which exploded beneath the rear of the jet. Seeing another F-105 flying directly in front of him, he fired his second missile and this exploded next to its left wing.

While my leader was attacking the No. 4 F-105, I chased the No. 2 aircraft on the right of the formation and fired a salvo of rockets that exploded behind the target. The F-105 then accelerated away to safety. Moments later, our command post ordered us to break off the engagement and return to base. After ending the pursuit, I saw the F-105 that had been hit by my leader burning fiercely, with a solitary parachute floating down nearby.

According to USAF records, only Capt R. B. Cooley's 357th TFS/355th TFW F-105D (60-0502) was shot down that day. Its demise was credited to Dong Van De.

The MiG-21s continued to claim victories during December by using the tactic of intercepting targets at long range and attacking from the same altitude with R-3Ss. VPAF Command soon issued orders stating that enemy aircraft were to be engaged at even greater ranges in an effort to disrupt attacks as they penetrated the outer perimeter of the North Vietnamese defenses.

From September 21 to December 19, the VPAF had many successful battles in which "Fishbed" pilots claimed ten F-105s destroyed – USAF records state just one was lost to a MiG-21, with an F-4C also being downed. These victories confirmed that the decision to use revised tactics was the correct one.

Although two "Fishbeds" had been lost to F-4Cs and one to an F-8E during this period, the successes credited to VPAF pilots using "fast pass" tactics in the final months of 1966 gave them the confidence to target aircraft at the center of large enemy strike formations and then quickly depart before the fighter escorts could react. Such attacks were of great tactical significance because they disrupted strike packages at long range, when fighter-bomber pilots were still finalizing their formations prior to making their runs into the target area. The presence of fast-flying MiG-21s forced pilots to jettison their bombs and abandon their planned attacks.

Overall, in 1966 the VPAF had flown 623 combat missions and engaged in 196 aerial battles, the latter resulting in claims being made for the destruction of 54 American aircraft. MiG-21 pilots had been credited with shooting down 20 of them, although US records state just four were destroyed by "Fishbeds." The VPAF acknowledged the loss of seven MiG-21s – six pilots had successfully ejected from their stricken aircraft and survived. There had been just one fatality.

The scene was now set for the bloodiest year of aerial combat during *Rolling Thunder*, with significant losses being suffered by both sides.

High-scoring aces Nguyen Van Coc (in the cockpit) and Pham Thanh Ngan use a wooden model of a MiG-21 to confirm which tactical formation they will employ upon departure from Noi Bai. Note that both pilots are wearing personal identification armbands. (István Toperczer Collection)

CHAPTER 6
COMBAT

US aircraft continued to attack powerplants, industrial sites, transport infrastructure, and military targets in the Hanoi and Haiphong areas through the dry season of 1967. They also hit AAA and SAM batteries in Viet Tri, Thai Nguyen, and Quang Ninh provinces as they tried to isolate Hanoi from Haiphong, and the two cities from other regions of the country. Attacks on MiG bases also limited the jets' operational capabilities. In response, the VPAF attempted to make the best use of its small fighter force by concentrating on the defence of Hanoi.

The new year started badly for the VPAF. On January 2, five MiG-21s were shot down (the USAF claimed seven destroyed) over Noi Bai, although all of the pilots involved managed to safely eject. At noon, a strike formation – part of a dedicated MiG-baiting operation codenamed *Bolo* – had entered North Vietnamese airspace led by World War II ace Col R. Olds, CO of the 8th TFW. The F-4Cs assigned to this special mission flew along the northern corridor of RP-6 at the same altitude and speed as F-105s. And like the Thunderchiefs they were trying to mimic, each jet carried an EW jamming pod in an attempt to fool North Vietnamese radar operators. Unlike the F-105s, the Phantom IIs were exclusively armed with AAMs.

Some of the F-4s flew in formation toward Noi Bai, while another group headed at low altitude for a holding position north of the Tam Dao mountains. The Noi Bai and Kep MiGs were at full combat alert. Cloud density was ten-tenths, with the base at 1,500m and the top at 3,000m. The VPAF central command post prevented the MiGs from taking off until the intruders were just 40km from Noi Bai, and by this time two flights of USAF fighters were waiting above the clouds.

At 1356 hrs the first MiG flight, comprising Vu Ngoc Dinh, Nguyen Duc Thuan, Nguyen Dang Kinh, and Bui Duc Nhu, took off. They quickly encountered four F-4s over Phu Ninh, with Dinh leading the pursuit. When the Phantom II crews reacted aggressively to his presence, he turned away. Dinh then spotted two more F-4s behind him just as they fired missiles at his MiG-21. It was too late for evasive action, and Dinh's aircraft ("Red 4222") was hit by an AIM-7E fired by 1Lts R. F. Wetterhahn and J. K. Sharp of the 555th TFS/8th TFW. The MiG became uncontrollable and Dinh ejected.

Le Trong Huyen uses models to brief (left to right) Nguyen Ngoc Do, Bui Duc Nhu, Nguyen Van Thuan, and Nguyen Dang Kinh. All four pilots being briefed would all be shot down by 8th TFW F-4C Phantom IIs during Operation *Bolo* on January 1967. (István Toperczer Collection)

Meanwhile, Kinh had joined up with Thuan and Nhu in chasing a flight of F-4s flying below them. Four of the enemy aircraft increased speed and fled, but Kinh sighted Olds' flight lying in wait above the cloud layer surrounding the Tam Dao mountains. When the Phantom IIs had maneuvered into an attack position, Olds (and his Weapon Systems Officer 1Lt C. C. Clifton) launched two Sparrow missiles and a Sidewinder at the MiG-21s. Kinh asked Thuan and Nhu for their current locations but received no reply. He then realized his aircraft ("Red 4126") had been hit and he decided to eject.

Thuan and Nhu had become separated from the Dinh–Kinh pairing and were soon embroiled in a dogfight of their own with the F-4s. The Phantom II crews fired so many missiles that both MiGs ("Red 4125" and "Red 4225") were hit. Thuan and Nhu also ejected safely. They had been shot down by the 555th TFS/8th TFW crews of Capt W. S. Radecker and 1Lt J. E. Murray and Capt E. T. Raspberry and 1Lt R. W. Western.

A similar fate would befall the leader of the second MiG-21 formation that had taken off from Noi Bai at the same time as Dinh's flight. After Nguyen Ngoc Do had led Dang Ngoc Ngu, Dong Van De, and Nguyen Van Coc through the clouds at an altitude of 3,000m, he sighted enemy aircraft and turned to port. Shortly thereafter, Do saw an F-4 fire two missiles at their MiGs. He in turn pursued the two leading Phantom IIs, firing a missile at them. Moments later Do felt his MiG ("Red 4029") become unstable, go into a side-slip and then drop into a spin. The jet had been hit by an AIM-7E fired by Capt J. B. Stone and 1Lt C. P. Dunnegan flying an F-4C from the 433rd TFS/8th TFW. Do ejected, while the remaining three "Fishbed" pilots broke off the engagement and returned to Noi Bai.

According to Vu Ngoc Dinh, VPAF Command had failed to realize that the USAF was about to organize a "sweep the skies" campaign specifically aimed at neutralizing the growing threat posed by the 921st FR:

> We were completely shocked. They [the Americans] studied the weather and the cloud cover above Noi Bai. They sent about 90 fighters disguised as fighter-bombers, which they divided into two groups. And they jammed everywhere they appeared, which made the whole sky become "dark" so that we could see nothing on the radar. When they were over Noi Bai disguised as fighter-bombers our radar finally detected them, and only then were two flights of eight MiGs ordered to take off – I led the first. We flew through solid cloud that went from 300m up to 3,000m. When we broke out of the overcast we encountered the F-4s that were waiting for us, and five of us were shot down. I felt so angry and indignant.

After that combat I was on standby in the afternoon, instead of going to the hospital. Of the five pilots who had ejected, I was the only one fit enough to be on standby. The rest had had to be hospitalized. The next day, when I finally got to be examined in the hospital, our commander, Phung The Tai, visited me and said, "It was our mistake." and then he left. The fact that a commander dared to admit his mistake made us respect and believe him. After this meeting, I felt reassured. In the afternoon I was on standby again.

On January 6, Col Olds devised a new tactic that would again inflict losses on the 921st FR. This time, he briefed F-4Cs of the 555th TFS/8th TFW to fly in tight formation along a flightpath regularly used by unarmed RF-4C reconnaissance aircraft photographing targets in Hanoi. After North Vietnamese radar had picked up the target, and concluded that it was a flight of reconnaissance aircraft, a GCI command post agreed to scramble MiG-21s at 0924 hrs. Tran Hanh, Mai Van Cuong, Dong Van De, and Nguyen Van Coc took off from Noi Bai and climbed through solid cloud in order to intercept what they believed were RF-4Cs. Coc explained what happened next:

That day, I was flying in the No. 4 position as wingman for Dong Van De [in the No. 3 jet]. Right after we broke through the top of the cloud layer I heard Mai Van Cuong [in the No 2 jet] report that he had spotted F-4s behind us. Tran Hanh also saw the enemy aircraft, and immediately realizing we had flown into a trap, he ordered the flight to turn hard to the right. De and I were still in the process of trying to form up after heading through the cloud in loose formation, which meant we were not yet able to make the turn.

Having pulled my control column hard over in order to turn inside my flight lead, I was able to see two missiles trailing white smoke flash beneath the belly of my MiG and head straight for De's jet ["Red 4025"], which was on the outside of the turn. I shouted "Eject! Eject! Eject!" and De left his jet. His ejection was not successful, however, and he did not survive.

Hanh ordered the flight to dive back through the cloud layer, and when I broke out below the undercast I found myself over the Tam Dao mountains. I saw a MiG diving toward the ground and I again shouted "Eject," but the aircraft crashed moments later. It turned out that Cuong had already ejected from his aircraft while he was still in cloud.

On January 6, 1967, future eight-victory ace Mai Van Cuong was forced to eject when his MiG-21PFL "Red 4023" was hit by a Sparrow missile fired from an F-4C of the 555th TFS/8th TFW. Cuong, who would also be shot down by a US Navy Phantom II ten months later, landed safely in the Viet Tri–Phu Tho area. (István Toperczer Collection)

Hanh and Coc were then ordered to return home, and they both made it safely back to Noi Bai. De's MiG-21 had been hit by an AIM-7 fired by Capt R. M. Pascoe and 1Lt N. E. Wells, while Cuong's "Red 4023" was brought down by a Sparrow fired by Maj T. M. Hirsch and 1Lt R. J. Strasswimmer.

Six MiG-21s had now been lost in just two engagements, and not a single enemy aircraft had been claimed in return. VPAF Command immediately suspended all combat operations by the 921st FR and ordered that tactics were to be thoroughly reviewed. Additional training was also conducted, with pilots drilled in hit-and-run "guerrilla-style" attacks using groups of two or four aircraft, with the attacking group's altitude and speed constantly changing. It was also decided that the MiG-21 pilots should strike enemy formations from above, while their counterparts in MiG-17s engaged fighter-bombers from the same altitude – preferably from either flank. This, it was hoped, would force the intruders into a turning dogfight.

The losses during *Bolo* effectively spelled the end for "Fishbed" operations in four-aircraft formations, with the VPAF choosing to use its MiG-21s as a "small and elite force" for the rest of *Rolling Thunder*. Following the disaster that befell the 921st FR in January 1967, the VPAF worked hard to improve interception techniques. GCI command posts were told that they needed to be more accurate in respect of timings when it came to scrambling MiG-21s.

Jets had to be airborne with sufficient time to allow pilots to target groups of fighter-bombers with a tactical advantage. This meant "Fishbeds" should intercept enemy aircraft with an approach angle of 30–45 degrees, a speed difference of 200–300km/h, and at an altitude 500–1,000m higher. The combination of these elements would help MiG-21 pilots with the early detection of enemy aircraft once in the air, which in turn meant they could position themselves for a "hit-and-run – deep penetration" attack and swift disengagement. Having been able to select the most vulnerable fighter-bomber formation as a target and engage it with AAMs immediately thereafter, pilots would then have sufficient time to flee before the escorts could counterattack.

Unlike the large aircraft formations that appeared near-daily over North Vietnam during *Rolling Thunder*, the MiG-21s tasked with intercepting them were always small in number, and each jet was usually equipped with just two AAMs. Unable to carry out a sustained attack, a VPAF pilot had to retreat as soon as his missiles had been fired. Following the *Bolo* debacle, aviators from the 921st FR had no choice but to penetrate deeply into large fighter-bomber formations once they had identified their target and then attack it with a "hit-and-run" pass. These new tactics would be successfully trialed from the summer of 1967. Their implementation, however, would have to wait awhile, as the badly mauled 921st was withdrawn until late April in an attempt to make good its losses.

North Korean Operations

Fortunately for the VPAF, the recent attrition it had suffered was partially offset by the arrival of aviators with MiG experience from North Korea. On September 21, 1966, in an effort to increase its pilot cadre as quickly as possible, the Vietnamese Central Military Party Committee led by Gen Vo Nguyen Giap had accepted the offer of a North Korean People's Air Force (NKPAF) regiment to fly MiG-17s and MiG-21s against the Americans. The USSR and China also offered pilots and jets to bolster the VPAF's campaign against US aircraft, but this was rejected by the North Vietnamese, who were anxious to avoid the conflict becoming a clash between Cold War superpowers. The agreement that was worked out between the VPAF and the NKPAF emphasized that the North Korean pilots involved were "specialists" who actually "volunteered" to participate in combat.

Officially, the unit was called Doan Z (Group Z), and it was stationed at Kep, northeast of Hanoi, from February 1967 through to early 1969 under

North Korean Doan Z and VPAF armorers prepare to equip ex-Cuban MiG-21F-13s with R-3S AAMs at Noi Bai in 1967. The first batch of "Fishbed-Cs" began arriving in Vietnam in June 1967 and, after assembly, were in combat-ready condition by the following month. NKPAF pilots routinely flew this variant from then on, often in four-aircraft formations. (István Toperczer Collection)

the command of Lt Col Kim Chang Xon. NKPAF pilots flew aircraft borrowed from the VPAF, specifically MiG-17s of the 923rd FR and MiG-21s of the 921st FR. Vu Ngoc Dinh, who occasionally flew with the Doan Z pilots, recalled:

> North Korea wanted to send aviators to Vietnam so that they could gain combat experience with the aim of bolstering the strength of the NKPAF. The pilots sent were their best ones, with parents or relatives working for the Politburo of the North Korean Central Party Committee. One of them was the son of Thoi Huu Kien, chairman of the North Korean National Assembly at the time.
>
> They sent their pilots and we provided the hardware they required during their service. They kept everything secret, so we didn't know their loss ratio, but the North Koreans claimed 26 American aircraft destroyed. Although they fought very bravely in the air, they were generally too slow and too mechanical in their reactions when engaged, which is why so many of them were shot down. They never followed instructions. I believe the North Koreans claimed four aerial victories with the aircraft.

The NKPAF pilots primarily engaged enemy aircraft over the provinces (Ha Bac, Vinh Phuc, and Hai Hung) near Hanoi. From March 1967, the names of North Korean pilots started to appear on the VPAF's official victory and loss lists. As noted by Vu Ngoc Dinh, the NKPAF sent its best pilots with high flying hours, and they were all captains or majors in rank. They often flew in pairs or four-aircraft formations, with the latter proving popular once the MiG-21F-13s became operational with the 921st FR in July 1967.

Despite their flying experience, the North Korean pilots did not impress their North Vietnamese counterparts in combat due to their inflexibility and disregard for instructions from GCI. They preferred the NR-30 cannon over AAMs, although most of their victories were scored with the "Atoll."

NKPAF pilots were particularly active in December 1967, and on the 16th 555th TFS/8th TFW F-4D 66-7631 flown by Korean War ace Maj J. F. Low and 1Lt H. J. Hill was downed by an AAM during an early morning CAP over Kep. The Phantom II was hit by an R-3S as the crew tried to escape from the area after running low on fuel during a lengthy dogfight. Both men ejected and were captured, their unnamed victor from Doan Z flying a MiG-21F-13.

Another victory for the unit came on January 5, 1968 when an *Iron Hand* flight from the 357th TFS/355th TFW lost F-105F *Wild Weasel* 63-8356 during a raid on a railway bridge at Dong Luc, near Kep. Maj J. C. Hartney and Capt S. Fantle, leading "Barracuda" flight, had just fired a Shrike anti-radiation missile when they were attacked by MiG-21F-13s. Cannon fire from one of the "Fishbed-Cs" hit the Thunderchief's port wing and it burst into flames. The crew ejected as the aircraft rolled out of control, but neither of them survived.

The final victory claimed by a NKPAF pilot came on February 12 when, at 1526 hrs, two MiG-21s were scrambled from Noi Bai to intercept a flight of F-4s detected heading for Tien Yen and Dinh Lap at an altitude of 7,000m. Kim Ki-hwan reported spotting two groups of Phantom IIs, totaling seven aircraft, below him. He attacked, and claimed one shot down, although his victory was not confirmed by USAF records.

As Kim attempted to break away following the interception, he was attacked by three MiGCAP (MiG Combat Air Patrol) F-4Ds from the 435th FS/8th FG. The flight lead crew of Lt Col A. E. Lang Jr and 1Lt R. P. Moss fired two AIM-7Es that hit the MiG-21 and sent it down in a violent, unrecoverable spin. Kim ejected, but did not survive.

Doan Z personnel returned to North Korea in early 1969.

Pilot Exhaustion

During April–May 1967, the VPAF's MiG bases were targeted for the first time as the USAF and US Navy initiated an intense bombing campaign against North Vietnamese targets. Forced to respond, the 921st FR flew 30 to 40 sorties per day, saturating the VPAF's GCI capability.

After 30 April, because the fighting had been so intense, the health of many of the MiG pilots had deteriorated and they had to be rested in order to recuperate. Due to a reduction in the number of MiG-17 pilots following significant combat attrition in the early months of 1967, VPAF Command had had to reduce the mission tempo of the "Fresco-C"-equipped 923rd FR. This in turn meant additional sorties, and losses, for the 921st FR. Amongst the pilots to be shot down was Nguyen Van Coc, who ejected from "Red 4325" after being engaged by Col R. Olds and 1Lt W. D. Lafever on May 4:

> I took off from Noi Bai with my leader, Pham Thanh Ngan. The enemy strike package was heading for Tam Dao ridge. We were flying at 350 degrees to it at an altitude of 2,000m. We discovered 12 F-105s in three flights and eight F-4s at a distance of seven kilometers. Ngan increased speed and attacked an F-105 on his left with an R-3S. He sighted three more Thunderchiefs and fired another missile from a distance of 1,200m. I didn't see any hits and Ngan broke off to land. I discovered four F-4s on my left and attacked them, but I soon heard a big bang behind my tailpipe. I'd been hit by an F-4 and had to return to Noi Bai. When my speed was 360km/h I turned the undercarriage control lever to "out." At an altitude of 100m my engine stopped, so I ejected. My MiG crashed 500m from the Noi Bai runway.

The unit lost two more MiG-21s on May 20, although in a day of considerable action the "Fishbed" pilots claimed a Phantom II destroyed. F-4Cs from the 433rd TFS/8th TFW were flying a MiGCAP mission for the Takhli-based F-105

Nguyen Nhat Chieu was credited with five victories between May 20 and October 19, 1967, having claimed his first success on September 20, 1965 in a MiG-17. He was among the first group of VPAF MiG pilots who trained to fly the MiG-17 in China between 1956 and 1964, prior to converting to the MiG-21 in Vietnam in 1966. (István Toperczer Collection)

strike force that was targeting the Bac Le railway marshaling yard when the escort fighters were engaged by 12 to 14 MiG-17s from Doan Z – four of the latter fell to the Phantom IIs.

As the F-4s and F-105s pressed on to their target, two MiG-21 pairs also attempted to attack them. At 1516 hrs Nguyen Nhat Chieu and Pham Thanh Ngan, joined four minutes later by Vu Ngoc Dinh and Nghiem Dinh Hieu, took off from Noi Bai and headed for Tam Dao. Detecting enemy aircraft on their left at a distance of eight kilometers, Chieu increased speed and fired an R-3S, but no result was observed. When Ngan warned him of enemy aircraft behind, Chieu performed a series of evasive maneuvers before spotting four Phantom IIs above him. Climbing to 3,500m, he fired another R-3S and downed the F-4C of Maj J. L. Loan and 1Lt J. E. Milligan.

At the same time the remaining MiG-21 pair was flying 15–20km behind Chieu and Ngan. Vu Ngoc Dinh recalled the battle that took place:

I spotted four F-4s and requested permission to attack, but the command post refused to permit me into our AAA unit's firing area. We joined up with Chieu to form a three-aircraft formation, and when I flipped my aircraft onto its left side to scan the area I saw four F-4s pursuing us. I shouted to Hieu to take immediate evasive action, then two missiles exploded on the right-hand side of my aircraft. I made quick evasive maneuvers and climbed to 7,000m. When I leveled out to change course, I saw two more F-4s flash over my head. I found that my aircraft was difficult to control, the hydraulic system having been seriously damaged. As I began to spiral downward there was a lot of smoke in the cockpit, so I decided to eject. I lost consciousness for a time and my parachute lines became tangled. I untangled them so the 'chute could open properly, and landed in Thanh Van village in Bac Thai Province.

Maj R. D. Janca and 1Lt W. E. Roberts of the 389th TFS/366th TFW had downed Dinh's MiG-21 ("Red 4321") with an AIM-9.

Meanwhile, Hieu had pulled up hard to the left following Dinh's warning, and he then spotted yet another pair of F-4s. He fired a missile at one and quickly broke off the engagement. At that moment Hieu's aircraft ("Red 4024") was hit by a Sparrow fired by Lt Col R. E. Titus and 1Lt M. Zimer, also of the 389th TFS/366th TFW. Hieu ejected but died on his way to hospital.

Shocked by recent heavy losses (39 MiG-17s and 15 MiG-21s were credited to American pilots between January 2 and June 5, 1967), the VPAF again drastically reduced MiG activity. From mid-June, a series of meetings were held to discuss what had gone wrong in recent weeks. While the enemy had improved its air combat tactics and switched to two-level formations when undertaking strike missions, the VPAF had continued to employ intercept procedures and maneuvers that had become outdated. Further discussion revealed other contributory causes, including poor intelligence of enemy plans, a lack of situational awareness amongst pilots involved in aerial engagements and no rapid post-mission review of combat experiences within the 921st.

Many pilots had underestimated their enemy's capabilities, and GCI command post officers had failed to provide adequate support for aviators attempting to intercept aircraft. It was also found that MiG-21 losses were high when the enemy conducted dedicated "sweep the sky" missions like *Bolo*. The MiG pilots also repeated the same mistakes over and over again when engaging the enemy, failing to adapt when the USAF modified its tactics in an effort to negate the growing MiG-21/R-3S threat. "Fishbed" pilots stuck rigidly to dogfighting in the same area for too long. They had also been fooled by the enemy's tactic of disguising fighters as strike aircraft. Many pilots had failed to undertake "hit-and-run" attacks, and the cooperation between MiG-17 and MiG-21 units was not considered sufficiently effective.

Nguyen Nhat Chieu used MiG-21PFL "Red 4228" to shoot down F-4D 66-0238 of the 555th TFS/8th TFW during aerial combat on August 23, 1967. The 555th lost no fewer than four Phantom IIs on this date during an attack on the Yen Vien railway marshaling yard, with two of the jets falling to the 921st FR. (István Toperczer Collection)

From August the 921st FR made a concerted effort to implement "hit-and-run" tactics. This certainly improved the unit's success rate, with US records acknowledging the loss of 13 F-4B/Ds and F-105D/Fs and a solitary RF-101C to MiG-21s between August 23 and December 17, 1967, compared with just four in the previous seven months – the VPAF credited the 921st with 49 victories in 1967. The new tactic had a significant impact on the "Fishbed's" victory–loss ratio, with the exchange ratio going from four-to-one in favor of US fighters to 3.6-to-one in favor of the MiG-21, according to VPAF records. In fact, the correct use of "hit-and-run" attacks saw the 921st FR virtually match its opponents victory-for-victory between August 1967 and February 1968.

The improved results enjoyed by the VPAF also demonstrated that the MiG-21 was capable of holding its own against the Phantom II if GCI techniques were implemented that played to the communist fighter's key strengths. As if to prove this point, on August 23 the 921st claimed three F-4Ds destroyed – the first examples of the new Phantom II variant to fall to the MiG-21.

That afternoon, radar stations reported a large package of 40 US aircraft south of Xam Neua, bound for the Yen Vien railway marshaling yard. At 1456 hrs Doan Z MiG-17 pilots took off from Kep, while their VPAF counterparts scrambled from Gia Lam. Two minutes later the MiG-21s of Nguyen Nhat Chieu ("Red 4228") and Nguyen Van Coc ("Red 4227") were scrambled from Noi Bai in order to intercept the enemy strike formation at long range. The pilots were directed to fly to the west and initially stay at low altitude. They eventually climbed to 6,000m and then headed north to intercept the USAF aircraft. At Tuyen Quang, Chieu detected F-4s and F-105s 15km away. Nguyen Van Coc recalled how the mission unfolded from there:

> Chieu and I went the long way around to get into a better position from which to attack. Chieu fired a missile, bringing down an F-4D, while I successfully attacked the other Phantom II, again with an R-3S. In the meantime, Chieu went after another jet. He then flew into cloud, only to reappear moments later. Following my leader, I also successfully attacked a Phantom II with a missile, but I was too close and came into

the line of Chieu's fire as he dived from above. Although my MiG-21 was damaged by his AAM, my controls operated normally. Although I requested to carry on with the engagement, the command post ordered me to return to base because of the damage, which restricted my MiG-21 to a maximum speed of 600km/h.

Chieu's victim had been the F-4D flown by Maj C. R. Tyler and Capt R. N. Sittner, while Coc's missile had struck the Phantom II of Capt L. E. Carrigan and 1Lt C. Lane. Both jets were from the 555th TFS/8th TFW. According to other sources, Coc had fired his missile at too close a range and debris from the American aircraft was ingested into his engine air intake. After landing, mechanics counted 51 pieces of the Phantom II stuck in the air intake cone.

When Chieu heard that Coc's aircraft had been damaged, he turned back to cover his comrade. Moments later Chieu spotted another formation of Phantom IIs and fired his second R-3S, hitting the 555th TFS/8th TFW F-4D of Maj R. R. Sawhill and 1Lt G. L. Gerndt – USAF records stated that this jet was struck by AAA. Chieu then escaped by flying into cloud, but not before he had rolled his aircraft onto its back to see three fires burning on the ground below him, marking the crash sites of the downed Phantom IIs.

As previously noted, in October there was a major change in US tactics when fighter-bombers started targeting MiGs on the ground in a concerted attempt to paralyze VPAF operations. One such attack on Noi Bai on the 24th destroyed five MiG-21s and seven MiG-17s. This offensive proved so effective that by year-end only around 20 MiGs (both types) were flying from North Vietnamese airfields, with the balance of the fleet operating from Chinese bases.

Nevertheless, the pilots that remained operational as part of a "small but elite" MiG force had by now become highly proficient in intercepting enemy fighter-bombers. They demonstrated their skills by consistently positioning themselves behind strike formations and then utilizing their superior height and speed to make an effective single attacking pass during which they fired AAMs.

This was indeed the case on November 18, when the 388th TFW attacked Noi Bai in poor weather in one of the first raids directed by the newly commissioned TSQ-81 bombing navigation radar site LS85 in northern Laos. Veteran pilots Pham Thanh Ngan and Nguyen Van Coc were on combat alert duty that day, and they had been instructed to attack the lead group of fighter-bombers tasked with suppressing the SAM sites and AAA batteries defending the airfield. Once ordered to take off, they flew to a holding area at Thanh Son. Here, they were told by GCI that their targets were 20km away, crossing from left to right. A few seconds later, both pilots detected four enemy aircraft in "finger-four" formation, with a wide distance between each jet.

Ngan (in "Red 4324") reported to command, "Targets detected, request permission to attack!" The controller replied, "Cleared! Be aware that there is a large enemy formation approaching behind these aircraft!" Ngan then ordered Coc (in "Red 4326") to "jettison external fuel tank, turn with afterburner engaged" and rolled right, following the target aircraft at transonic speed. He focused on attacking these jets, ignoring the aircraft behind him. He then radioed Coc again. "Attention No. 2. I'll attack the two aircraft on the left, you attack the pair on the right!"

On November 8, 1967, ace-to-be Dang Ngoc Ngu claimed his fourth aerial victory when he shot down 555th TFS/8th TFW F-4D 66-0250 flown by Maj W. S. Gordon and 1Lt R. C. Brenneman over the Phu Yen–Yen Bai area. Ngu trained to fly the MiG-17 between 1961–65 and converted to the MiG-21 in the Soviet Union in 1965–66. His service with the 921st FR began in 1966, and VPAF records credit him with seven aerial victories prior to his death in combat on July 8, 1972. (István Toperczer Collection)

Ngan targeted the No. 4 aircraft, *Wild Weasel* F-105F 63-8295 (call-sign "Waco 1") of the 34th TFS/388th TFW, flown by Maj O. M. Dardeau and Capt E. W. Lehnhoff. Having fatally damaged it with an R-3S, he then turned his attention to a second Thunderchief. However, due to his high closing speed and close proximity to his target, Ngan had to break off quickly to avoid a collision, and thus did not observe whether he had hit his second target. Coc, though, saw the F-105 struck by Ngan's missile, although it was only damaged by the missile.

Ngan then spotted more enemy aircraft behind him, so he increased his speed and climbed to 7,000m. Coc, meanwhile, pursued F-105D 60-0497 (call-sign "Waco 4") of the 469th TFS/388th TFW, this aircraft being flown by wing vice-commander Lt Col W. N. Reed. He fired a single R-3S at the fighter-bomber and saw it damaged when the missile exploded. Reed nursed the Thunderchief as far as Laos, where he ejected. The two MiG-21 pilots were then ordered to break off the engagement and head for Nanning airfield in China's Guangxi Province. However, the weather was so bad there that they had to head to Kep.

1458 hrs, AUGUST 23, 1967

PHU THO PROVINCE

1 MiG-21PFLs "Red 4227" and "Red 4228" of the 921st FR are scrambled from Noi Bai to intercept USAF fighter-bomber formations crossing the border bound for the Yen Vien railway marshaling yard in Hanoi. To avoid detection by the USAF jets, Nguyen Nhat Chieu (in "Red 4228") and Nguyen Van Coc (in "Red 4227") remain at low-level until they are within visual distance of the enemy formations, at which point they zoom-climb in afterburner to 6,000m and intercept the approaching jets from the left at an angle of 60 degrees.

2 As they jettison their centerline tanks and prepare to engage the third formation of F-4Ds from above and behind, Coc, flying as wingman to Chieu, radios his leader to tell him he has spotted a new group of enemy aircraft flying some way behind the third formation. Chieu duly opts to attack the fourth formation instead.

3 Banking to the left, Chieu and Coc drop in behind the fourth formation of eight F-4Ds from the 555th TFS/8th TFW and ready their R-3S AAMs for a textbook rear hemisphere attack.

4 Chieu fires first, hitting 66-0238 flown by Maj C. R. Tyler and Capt R. N. Sittner.

5 Having covered his leader's successful attack, Coc moves up to within 1,000m of the Phantom II on the far right of the formation, locks his missile's seeker head onto the enemy jet and fires his R-3S.

6 Coc's missile hits 66-0247, flown by Capt L. E. Carrigan and 1Lt C. Lane, and the resulting explosion sees "Red 4227" peppered with debris as its pilot veers away from the disintegrating F-4D.

7 Despite the MiG's intake having suffered extensive damage, Coc evades the remaining Phantom IIs and is escorted back to Noi Bai by Chieu. As the latter covers his wingman's landing, two F-4Ds streak across his nose, unaware of the two "Fishbeds" on short finals.

8 While Coc lands safely, Chieu accelerates into a right banking turn and takes a shot with his one remaining R-3S at 66-0726, flown by Maj R. R. Sawhill and 1Lt G. L. Gerndt. He then makes another banking turn to the right and loses his pursuers in nearby cloud cover.

FOLLOWING PAGES

1
3
2
4
5

4228
6
7
8
4228

MiG-21PFL "Red 4326" participated in numerous aerial battles between September and November 1967, with its various pilots claiming a total of 13 victories in the aircraft. Its final success was credited to Nguyen Van Coc on November 18, 1967 when he mortally damaged F-105D 60-0497 of the 469th TFS/388th TFW. By then, the number of operational MiG-21s had drastically decreased, forcing pilots to fly whatever jet was serviceable. This often meant a formation leader would sortie in a MiG-21PFL while his wingman flew a MiG-21F-13 like "Red 4528," seen here preparing to taxi out from the flightline at Noi Bai. (István Toperczer Collection)

In early December 1967, the VPAF demonstrated its increased GCI capability by simultaneously engaging enemy strike packages with both MiG-21s and MiG-17s. They would attack from different directions in multiple waves in an attempt to confuse the MiGCAP formations. On the 17th, for example, a "Fresco-C" flight assisted three MiG-21s in attacking a formation of F-105s and F-4s targeting the Lang Lau railway bridge.

On this occasion, the 921st FR decided to test a new formation consisting of three MiG-21s, Vu Ngoc Dinh, Nguyen Dang Kinh, and Nguyen Hong Nhi (the latter having taken off alone from Noi Bai shortly after Dinh and Kinh) being given the job of undertaking a coordinated attack with MiG-17s. The latter would keep the MiGCAP busy while the 921st FR pilots went after the Thunderchiefs. Vu Ngoc Dinh recalled:

> When our radar sites detected electronic jamming signals along the flightpath approaching Hanoi from the west, the GCI command post ordered us to take off. We headed toward Hoa Binh, climbing to an altitude of 6,000m. As we flew past Phu Tho, we spotted six flights of F-105s and F-4s heading from Thailand to Tam Dao to attack Hanoi. They were stretched out in a long line that seemed to darken the whole sky.
>
> I decided to bypass the F-4 MiGCAP and target the F-105s out in front. I instructed Kinh to "Attack immediately, together!," aiming my jet at the middle of their formation. The F-105 pilots realized that they were being chased by our MiGs and immediately pulled up into a climb, before pushing over into a dive. It was at that point I pressed the missile firing button, releasing an AAM that struck its target. The F-105 fell away toward the ground in the Thai Nguyen area.
>
> I then maneuvered onto the tail of a second F-105, leveled off behind my target and fired my second missile. It too registered a hit. Now out of weapons, I broke off my attack by climbing up to an altitude of 10,000m, from where I flew to the airfield at Gia Lam.

While the strike package was seeking to make good its escape after having been attacked by both MiG-17s and MiG-21s, Nguyen Hong Nhi was ordered to take off. He was tasked with making a follow-up attack on the surviving F-105s, which were still in a state of confusion following their interception by Dinh. As he flew past Thanh Son, Nhi spotted eight Thunderchiefs below him some 10–15km away. Diving in behind the aircraft, he quickly closed in on his target and fired an R-3S that he claimed hit the fighter-bomber and set it on fire – USAF records fail to corroborate the kill, however.

As Nhi broke away in a turning climb, he spotted 16 more F-105s heading for Hanoi. Engaging full afterburner and quickly closing to within interception range, he then attempted to fire his second missile but the R-3S failed to launch. Nhi broke off the chase with a "split-S" maneuver and headed back to Noi Bai. Just short of the airfield, he ran into another formation of F-105s. Nhi quickly latched onto the tail of a Thunderchief, but the faulty AAM again refused to fire. Reluctantly, he turned away and landed at Noi Bai.

During this action the three MiG-21 pilots had successfully coordinated their attacks with each other, determining the correct targets to engage while the MiG-17s took on the MiGCAP. Although the 921st FR claimed three F-105s destroyed, USAF records only confirmed the loss of Vu Ngoc Dinh's first victim – F-105D 60-0422 of the 469th TFS/388th TFW, with its pilot, 1Lt J Thomas Ellis, being captured.

The engagement on December 17 revealed just how far the VPAF had come during 1967 in respect of the tactics it was now prepared to employ when intercepting strike packages. Two MiG-21s and four MiG-17s had overwhelmed the MiGCAP and the fighter-bombers they were supposed to be protecting

1500 hrs, JANUARY 3, 1968

PHU THO PROVINCE

1 With US strike aircraft targeting the Kinh No railway marshaling yard in large numbers, "Red 5030" (the only serviceable MiG-21PFM then at Noi Bai), with Ha Van Chuc at the controls, is sent aloft to intercept them.

2 Once over Yen Chau, Chuc spots a large formation of F-105s from the 388th TFW, and their F-4 escorts, heading for Kinh No. The USAF jets are in three groups, each numbering 36 aircraft, in an extended trail formation. Chuc requests permission to attack.

3 Seeing the rear MiGCAP escort of four F-4s turning to engage him head-on, Chuc banks to the right to engage the lead formation of F-105s.

4 However, his high closing speed prevents him firing his missiles and he quickly flies past the second and third Thunderchief formations.

5 Responding as briefed should they be targeted by MiGs, elements of the lead F-105 formation jettison their bombs and turn to pursue the "Fishbed" as it flies overhead.

6 With both F-4s and F-105s in hot pursuit, Chuc pulls his fighter into a high-G turn in order to place his jet behind the rear section of bombed-up Thunderchiefs. From here, he can mount an effective attack with his R-3S missiles.

7 With the lead Thunderchief no more than 1,000m ahead of him, Chuc locks his AAM onto its tailpipe and fires. The weapon hits F-105D 58-1157, flown by Col J. E. Bean, the fighter-bomber erupting in flames and falling away. The remaining three jets in the formation immediately split up. Chuc then makes good his escape in full afterburner while the Thunderchiefs are targeted by SAMs.

FOLLOWING PAGES

1
5030
5003
4
3
5
2

6
5030
7
JV

with a series of near simultaneous attacks from either side and slightly above the strike package. A third lone "Fishbed" had then harassed F-105s as they pressed on to the target. Such coordinated interceptions would continue in 1968.

During the afternoon of January 3, 1968, Ha Van Chuc downed F-105D 58-1157 west of Thai Nguyen. Its pilot was Col J. E. Bean, deputy of operations for the 388th TFW, who ejected into captivity. Chuc was flying MiG-21PFM "Red 5030," and his success was one of three victories claimed by "Fishbed-F" pilots that day – the first for this variant in VPAF service. (István Toperczer Collection)

New Year, More Action

The new year started as the old one had finished. On the morning of January 3, a large formation of enemy aircraft was detected by radar in the northwest region. Two MiG-21s flown by Nguyen Dang Kinh and Bui Duc Nhu took off from Noi Bai and headed for Thanh Son. Kinh sighted the bomb-laden F-105s flying ahead of the F-4 escorts and he immediately launched an R-3S that he claimed hit a Thunderchief. Nhu quickly followed suit, shooting down another F-105 at very close range. Neither loss was confirmed by official USAF records, however.

The raiders returned in the afternoon when 36 aircraft were reported flying over Yen Chau heading for the Kinh No railway marshaling yard. During the ensuing battle, Ha Van Chuc downed Col J. E. Bean's 469th TFS/388th TFW F-105D (58-1157) west of Thai Nguyen. Chuc claimed a further success on the 14th when he intercepted Maj S. H. Horne's Thunderchief (60-0489, again from the 469th TFS/388th TFW) east of Yen Bai airfield. However, Chuc's MiG-21 was also damaged in the engagement – there were no "Fishbed" claims made by USAF pilots on this date – and he sustained wounds from which he died five days later.

January 14 also saw the 921st finally claim a highly prized EB-66, which this time was confirmed by the USAF – indeed, it was the only Destroyer that was listed as downed by a MiG. VPAF radar detected an EB-66 at an altitude of 8,840m accompanied by a large formation of F-4s and F-105s over Route No. 15 (part of the Ho Chi Minh Trail). A pair of MiG-21s was scrambled from Noi Bai and at 1547 hrs Nguyen Dang Kinh and Dong Van Song located the Destroyer at a range of 12km. Kinh launched two R-3Ss at the EW aircraft but without any result. Song then closed on the EB-66C (55-0388) and fired a single missile that hit its starboard engine. The aircraft, from the 355th TFW's 41st Tactical Electronic Warfare Squadron, crashed 65km west of Thanh Hoa.

By the end of January the 921st FR was facing a shortage of pilots and aircraft, and it was forced to resort to a "two-plus-one" formation, rather than sending four jets aloft. The third MiG-21 would fly above and behind a two-aircraft formation, giving the lone pilot a better field-of-view so that he could spot targets and provide interception information to the remaining jets.

The lack of available aircraft also resulted in the VPAF flying a series of single jet sorties in February. The lone "Fishbed" would be directed in the general vicinity of an incoming strike package and the pilot engaged enemy jets from above with an altitude advantage of 1,500–3,000m. The loose vectoring of the MiG-21 toward target aircraft rather than precise positioning for an attack by GCI indicated that the pilot was being given the option as to which flight he engaged. It also allowed him to initiate the attack from the forward or rear quadrant.

In the first half of 1968, 33 newly qualified MiG-21 pilots returned from the Soviet Union, and they were immediately posted to the 921st FR. The

USSR also supplied the VPAF with 36 MiG-21PFMs during this period, and some of these aircraft were destroyed on the ground in airfield attacks.

Following the hectic start to the new year, the number of aerial engagements fought in the early spring drastically decreased due to the dwindling stock of serviceable MiG-21s. By the end of April the 921st FR had just four combat-ready MiG-21PFLs and ten MiG-21F-13s, with the new MiG-21PFMs suffering from technical issues that prevented them from being flown operationally. In some cases, mixed flights were sortied, with the leader in a "Fishbed-D" and his wingman in a "Fishbed-C."

MiG-21PFM "Red 5013" heads a row of "Fishbed-Fs" at Noi Bai toward the end of *Rolling Thunder*. This aircraft was used to claim victories over a US Navy RA-5C (the 90th, and last, victory credited to a MiG by US records) and an F-4 on December 28, 1972, although it was in turn shot down during the same mission by an F-4J from VF-142. The jet behind it, "Red 5015," was camouflaged with dark green spots over light green uppersurfaces prior to being based at Tho Xuan during the summer and fall of 1968. (István Toperczer Collection)

The crisis afflicting the VPAF's fighter force was eased somewhat on March 31 when President Lyndon B. Johnson announced the first in a series of bombing restrictions. This came into effect the following day, when all raids north of the 20th parallel (roughly midway through RP-4) were halted. On April 3 the bombing line was moved further south to the 19th parallel, thus restricting strikes to RP-1, RP-2 and in the southern third of RP-3.

With the introduction of these restrictions, the focus of operations for the Seventh Air Force and TF 77 shifted away from Hanoi and Haiphong to Military District No. 4 in the south of the country. USAF and US Navy aircraft now started targeting the area from Lam River in Nghe An Province to Gianh

MiG MASTER

By the end of January 1968, the 921st FR was experiencing such a severe shortage of pilots and aircraft that it was forced to sortie "two-plus-one" formations, rather than a pair of two-ships. As a result, on February 3, Pham Thanh Ngan and Nguyen Van Coc took off three times to intercept enemy aircraft, while Mai Van Cuong flew a series of diversionary sorties. That morning, they were scrambled to counter flights of F-4s, but the subsequent combat was inconclusive. In the afternoon, radar detected two enemy aircraft approaching from the south of Moc Chau. Ngan and Coc took off for a third time and headed for Hoa Binh, while Mai Van Cuong flew a diversionary sortie toward Thanh Son. At 1550 hrs the MiG-21 pair turned south for Quy Chau, whereupon the pilots sighted the target near Hoi Xuan at an altitude of 9,500m. The MiGs were at 10,500m when Ngan reported the presence of an "EB-66" just five kilometers away over Que Phong, on the border with Laos. He banked to the left and discovered not the expected Destroyer but a pair of F-102A Delta Daggers from the 509th FIS/405th FW, these aircraft occasionally flying CAPs for air strikes.

Maj A. L. Lomax in the lead interceptor turned and fired three AIM-4D Falcon AAMs at the MiGs, but they all missed. Meanwhile, Ngan had maneuvered into a firing position behind Lomax's wingman, 1Lt W. L. Wiggins. He attempted to launch a missile but the R-3S failed to leave the rail. Ngan immediately launched his second AAM and downed 1Lt Wiggins' F-102A 56-1166. He then pulled up into a right-hand climb so that he could watch, and cover, his wingman's attack on the remaining Delta Dagger. Coc duly fired a missile at Lomax's jet, but it failed to guide correctly. The MiG-21s were then ordered to break off the engagement. Wiggins' Delta Dagger was the only example downed by the VPAF during the conflict.

River in Quang Binh Province. In the wake of this operational change, VPAF Command formulated a plan for the defense of the supply routes in Military District No 4. It established headquarters at Hanoi, Gia Lam, and Noi Bai, with support stations at Hoa Lac, Kien An, and Tho Xuan airfields. VPAF Command also ordered engineer units to repair Tho Xuan (in Thanh Hoa Province), with the aim of basing MiG-17s and MiG-21s there to cover the southern front.

In early April, the VPAF's Commander-in-Chief, Nguyen Van Tien, and other high ranking officers arrived in Military District No. 4 to study the weather, receive briefings on enemy tactics, review the state of airfields in this area, and check on the preparations being made to allow MiGs to be stationed there. Tho Xuan was opened shortly thereafter, and the few serviceable aircraft were regularly subjected to temporary deployments at Noi Bai, Gia Lam, Kep, Hoa Lac, Kien An, Tho Xuan, and Vinh according to operational requirements. There were communication and control centers all the way from Tho Xuan to Quang Binh, which vastly improved the command system in Military District No. 4. Command teams were organized at Tho Xuan, Vinh, and Anh Son airfields, manned by officers of the 921st and 923rd FRs. Tho Xuan airfield was also expanded to serve as a main base for the MiGs. With everything now in place, VPAF Command ordered the 921st FR to base three MiG-21s at Tho Xuan and undertake some "test" aerial battles to see how prepared the GCI facilities in the area really were.

When hitting targets in Military District No. 4, enemy aircraft operated under the guidance and control of their own land-based radar sites in Laos and South Vietnam, as well as shipborne radar on US Navy vessels sailing off the coast. This meant attacking jets flying from carriers on *Yankee Station* could quickly change their tactics when MiGs were detected nearby. They made sudden attacks on targets in the area and, when they met MiGs, jettisoned their bombs and retreated toward the sea. They also used small formations of aircraft to conduct low-altitude early morning raids on various local airfields, these strikes being generated in an attempt to force the MiG units to abandon their bases and head back north.

In respect of operations in Military District No. 4, VPAF pilots also had to endure GCI difficulties in this area throughout the conflict due to the topography of central Vietnam. The US Navy exploited the Gulf of Tonkin by positioning search radar-equipped warships off the coast of central North Vietnam that could not only detect airborne VPAF aircraft across all of Military District No. 4, but also shoot them down with their SAMs if they strayed too near. Flying time in this area had to be restricted and all airfields continued to be subjected to repeated bombing.

The 921st FR increased training in low flying and low-altitude interception in an effort to negate the effectiveness of shipborne radar, the regiment also changing the standard MiG-21 combat formation from a two-ship to "two-plus-

The VPAF often had to resort to using a "two-plus-one" formation when operating over Military District No. 4. Here, the VPAF's three leading MiG-21 aces (Nguyen Hong Nhi, Pham Thanh Ngan, and Nguyen Van Coc) conduct an impromptu briefing for just such a mission in the spring of 1968. (István Toperczer Collection)

one." Pilots were encouraged to use their initiative, and they were given more information about enemy locations using codes and other secret communications methods. Radio silence was imposed from the time aircraft took off, pilots having to set their radios to receive mode only. If they sighted the enemy visually at ranges as close as 10–15km, they could use their radios.

In early May, three MiG-21s flown by Dang Ngoc Ngu, Nguyen Van Coc, and Nguyen Van Minh were sent covertly from Noi Bai to Tho Xuan. On the 7th, Nguyen Dang Kinh and Nguyen Van Lung left Noi Bai in their MiG-21s to fly a diversionary mission toward Anh Son in Military District No. 4. At the same time Ngu and Coc took off from Tho Xuan and flew at low altitude alongside Route No. 15 in the direction of Do Luong. The latter explained what happened next:

> Because of poor coordination with our assigned GCI command post, our MiGs were mistaken for American fighters and friendly AAA opened up on us. But this wasn't the only mistake, as Ngu also mistook Kinh and Lung for American jets. Preparing for an attack, Ngu dropped his fuel tank, but soon recognized the aircraft as North Vietnamese. We circled three times over Do Luong before we were informed about actual American fighters approaching from the sea. Ngu sighted two F-4s on our right and, due to very cloudy weather, he had to make a tight turn to attack. He was unable to get into a firing position, however.
>
> I couldn't follow him and was left seven kilometers behind. I made three banking turns in search of the enemy fighters, but by now I was running low on fuel. Rolling to the right, I turned in the direction of Tho Xuan. At that very moment I spotted an F-4 directly ahead of me at an altitude of 1,000–1,500m. The enemy pilot also saw me and turned in my direction. We then tried to get onto each other's tail in order to fire an AAM, performing two turning scissors maneuvers. When my opponent realized he could not get behind me, he suddenly leveled out and accelerated in the direction of the coast. I guessed he wanted to drag me out to sea and then break away to let a Talos missile-armed warship shoot my MiG down.
>
> My regimental deputy commander, Tran Hanh, at the GCI command post then told me "I can see the jet clearly. Continue your attack, and destroy the enemy aircraft!" I closed on the F-4 and, at a distance of 1,500m, heard the missile lock tone that indicated my AAMs were ready to go. I fired both "Atolls" just to make sure of the kill – when I pushed the button to launch the second missile, I could already see that the F-4 had been hit, as it was trailing flames. The jet crashed into the sea and I returned to Tho Xuan.

Coc had shot down F-4B BuNo 151485 of Lt Cdr E. S. Christensen and Lt(jg) W. A. Kramer of VF-92, which was embarked in USS *Enterprise* (CVAN-65). Following a confused action that had lasted 20 minutes, the MiG ace had bounced the Phantom II from the rear as its crew headed for the sea alone after they had run low on fuel following the dogfight with Coc and Ngu. The F-4's demise represented the VPAF's first aerial victory over Military District No. 4. This battle also revealed to the Americans that MiG-21s were now operating in this area. Consequently, US Navy units reviewed their tactics, revising the size of their attack formations and increasing the number of F-4s assigned to suppress the aerial threat.

Following the engagement on May 7, MiG-21 pilots lacked the element of surprise in Military District No. 4. Now when the MiGs approached US Navy strike packages, the enemy aircraft retreated. Furthermore, the MiG-21s had insufficient fuel for a viable pursuit of fleeing jets.

When, on May 23, "Fishbeds" again ventured south of the 19th parallel in force, they found a situation very similar to that under which American fighter-bombers had been operating for much of *Rolling Thunder*. The MiG-21s were operating at a considerable distance from their airfields, their GCI was unable to provide them with complete radar coverage, and there was now a very real SAM threat in the form of the ship-based RIM-8 Talos. That day, Ha Quang Hung's MiG-21F-13 was hit by just such a weapon fired from USS *Long Beach* (CGN-9) 105km away as he and Nguyen Van Coc were flying from Noi Bai to Tho Xuan. He ejected and then free-fell 4,000m before opening his parachute. Three more MiG-21s would fall to Talos missiles on September 22, because their pilots were not sufficiently wary of the ships' SAM capability and VPAF radar was not sophisticated enough to detect the missiles in order to warn them.

Nevertheless, VPAF fighter regiments continued to operate from Tho Xuan through to October 31, when *Rolling Thunder* finally came to an end. During this time they fought a number of aerial battles against intruding US Navy aircraft as they defended the strategic supply routes. The 921st FR participated in 20 aerial actions from June 16 to the end of the campaign in Military District No. 4, with MiG-21 pilots claiming 12 enemy aircraft destroyed for the loss of seven "Fishbeds" – US records state that just one aircraft was destroyed by a MiG-21 in the final six months of 1968. Four "Fishbeds" were shot down by US Navy fighters in return.

During the course of the year the 921st FR had not only helped defend Hanoi, it had also taken an active part in protecting ground transport moving through Military District No. 4. The US Navy, however, considered the MiG-21s less effective when operating this far south, so it did not attach special importance to them. It was true that the VPAF had encountered problems in the area because of the proximity of aircraft carriers and SAM-armed warships, as well as the topography of a region hemmed in by mountains on one side and the sea on the other. The weather was also unpredictable.

Despite being routinely outnumbered by enemy aircraft throughout *Rolling Thunder*, MiG-21 pilots had gained valuable combat experience in 1966–68 and inflicted notable losses on their opponents. Indeed, analysis of victory and loss lists from the VPAF and the USAF and US Navy reveals that the 921st FR achieved a 1.7-to-1 kill ratio in its favor during this period.

Nguyen Van Coc reads an article in the *National Army* newspaper detailing his success over Military District No. 4 on May 7. To his right are Ha Quang Hung (far left) and Nguyen Ngoc Thien (center). On May 23, Coc and Hung were flying from Noi Bai to Tho Xuan when Hung's MiG-21F-13 was hit by a RIM-8 Talos SAM fired from the cruiser *Long Beach* sailing in the Gulf of Tonkin, some 105km away. Having successfully ejected, he landed near Yen Thanh, in Nghe An Province. *(István Toperczer Collection)*

SELECTED SOURCES

Books published in Vietnam

Lich Su Khong Quan Nhan Dan Viet Nam (1955–1977) (People's Army, 1993)

Lich Su Dan Duong Khong Quan (1959–2004) (People's Army, 2004)

Lich Su Trung Doan Khong Quan 921 (1964–2009) (People's Army, 2009)

Lich Su Quan Chung Phong Khong – Khong Quan (1963–2013) (People's Army, 2012)

Chan Dung Anh Hung Phi Cong Thoi Ky Chong My Cuu Nuoc (National Cultural Publishing, 2012)

Nguyen Sy Hung and Nguyen Nam Lien, *Nhung Tran Khong Chien Tren Bau Troi Viet Nam (1965–1975) Nhin Tu Hai Phia* (People's Army, 2014)

Ky Yeu Phi Cong Tiem Kich Viet Nam Trong Khang Chien Chong My, Cuu Nuoc (1964–1973) (People's Army, 2017)

Nguyen Duc Soat and Nguyen Sy Hung, *Chien Tranh Tren Khong O Viet Nam (1965–1973) Phia Sau Nhung Tran Khong Chien* (People's Army, 2017)

Pham Phu Thai, *Linh Bay* (Writers' Association, 2017)

Books published elsewhere

Davies, Peter E., *Osprey Combat Aircraft 84 – F-105 Thunderchief Units of the Vietnam War* (Osprey Publishing, 2010)

Davies, Peter E., *Osprey Duel 12 – F-4 Phantom II vs MiG-21, USAF & VPAF in the Vietnam War* (Osprey Publishing, 2008)

Davies, Peter E., *Osprey Combat Aircraft 116 – US Navy F-4 Phantom II Units of the Vietnam War 1964–68* (Osprey Publishing, 2016)

Davies, Peter E., *Osprey Combat Aircraft 132 – F-102 Delta Dagger Units* (Osprey Publishing, 2020)

Mersky, Peter., *Osprey Combat Aircraft 7 – F-8 Crusader Units of the Vietnam War* (Osprey Publishing, 1998)

Futrell, R. Frank et al, *Aces and Aerial Victories – The United States Air Force in Southeast Asia 1965–1973* (Office of Air Force History, 1976)

Hobson, Chris, *Vietnam Air Losses* (Midland Publishing, 2001)

McCarthy, Donald J., *MiG Killers – A Chronology of US Air Victories in Vietnam 1965–1973* (Specialty Press, 2009)

Toperczer, István, *Osprey Combat Aircraft 29 – MiG-21 Units of the Vietnam War* (Osprey Publishing, 2001)

Toperczer, István, *MiG Aces of the Vietnam War* (Schiffer Publishing, 2015)

Toperczer, István, *Silver Swallows and Blue Bandits – Air Battles over North Vietnam 1964–1975* (Artipresse, 2015)

Toperczer, István, *Osprey Aircraft of the Aces 135 – MiG-21 Aces of the Vietnam War* (Osprey Publishing, 2017)

Documentary Sources

Red Baron Reports: Air-to-Air Encounters in Southeast Asia Vol I – Account of F-4 and F-8 Events Prior to March 1967 (Institute for Defence Analyses Systems Evaluation Division, October 1967)

Red Baron Reports: Air-to-Air Encounters in Southeast Asia Vol II – F-105 Events Prior to March 1967 (Institute for Defence Analyses Systems Evaluation Division, September 1968)

Red Baron Reports: Air-to-Air Encounters in Southeast Asia Vol III – Events from 1 March 1967 to 1 August 1967 and Miscellaneous Events (Institute for Defence Analyses Systems Evaluation Division, February 1969)

Project Red Baron II, Vols II to IV – Air-to-Air Encounters in Southeast Asia (USAF Tactical Fighter Weapons Center, January 1973)

Project Red Baron III, Vols I to III – Air-to-Air Encounters in Southeast Asia (USAF Tactical Fighter Weapons Center, June 1974)

INDEX

Note: references to images are in bold.

Abbott, Capt J. S. 7–8
Abbott, 1Lt R. A. 6
aircraft, North Vietnamese: MiG-17 "Fresco" 11, 22; see also MiG-21 "Fishbed"
aircraft, US 11–12, 27–28, 30
  Delta Dagger 73, **74–75**
"Alkali" missile 30, 47
Ammon, Capt G. L. 39
Andrews, Capt W. R. 40
Anh Son 21
"Atoll" missile 36–40

Bagley, Maj B. R. 18
Bean, Col J. E. 19
Bellinger, Cdr R. M. 33, **34–35**
Bieu, Hoang 54
Broughton, Col J. M. 7
bunkers 21

cannons 27–28, **29**, 30
Cao Bang 19
Caras, Capt F. A. 27–28
Cat Bi 19
Cay, Pham Minh 4
Chieu, Nguyen Nhat 24, 32, 40, 54
  and exhaustion 62, 63–66, 65, **66–67**
China 9, 14, 19, 36, 59
Chuc, Ha Van 19, 69, **70–71**, 72
Coc, Nguyen Van 4–7, 37–38, 54–55, 63–65, **66–67**
  and Bolo 57–58
  and diversionary sorties 73, **74–75**, 76–78
  and training 23–24
Cooley, Capt R. B. 55
Cuong, Mai Van 28, 42, 54, 58, 73, **74–75**

De, Dong Van 54–55, 57, 58
Dien Bien 19
Dinh, Vu Ngoc 7–8, 25, 28, 33, 36
  and Bolo 56–58
  and ejection 42
  and exhaustion 62, 68–69
  and NKPAF 60
  and targets 52–54
Do, Nguyen Ngoc 4–7, 18, 24, 57
Do Son 19
Dobson, Maj E. 7
Dong Hoi 19
Dunnegan, 1Lt C. P. 57

ejection seat 15, 22, **24**, 40–42
Ellis, 1Lt J. Thomas 69

Fantle, Capt S. 60

Gia Lam 19–21
Giap, Gen Vo Nguyen 59
Gilmore, Maj P. J. 46

Haiphong 11, 16
Hanh, Tran 4, **19**, 24, 58
Hanoi 4–5, 11
Hartney, Maj J. C. 60
Hieu, Nghiem Dinh 52–53, 62
Hoa Lac 19–20
Hung, Ha Quang 26
Huyen, Le Trong 7–8, 24, 28, 39, 52–53

interception 43–44, 46, 48, 50–51

Janca, Maj R. D. 62
Johnson, Capt H. E. 6
Johnson, Lyndon B. 73

Kep 19–21
Kien An 19–21
Kim Chang Xon, Lt Col 60
Kim Ki-hawn 61
Kinh, Bui Dinh 40, 69, 52, 72
Kinh, Nguyen Dang 18–19, 25, 46, 53, 68
  and Bolo 56, 57
  and diversionary sorties 77
  and ejection 42
Kinh, Nguyen Danh 40
Klause, K. J. 52
Korean War (1950–53) 12

Lafever, 1Lt W. D. 61
Lai Chau 19
Lan, Pham Ngoc 24
Lang Son 19
Lao Cai 19
Laos 18
Latham, 1Lt W. J. 52
Lenski, Maj A. 7–8
Long Beach, USS 78
Lung, Nguyen Van 77
Luong, Tran Thien 39, 52–53
Luyen, Dao Dinh 17, 24

McClelland, Maj William 36
maneuvers 43–44, **45**, 46, 48, 50
Manh, Tran 4–5, 24–25
MiG-21 "Fishbed" 11–16
  and bases 19–21
  and cannon 27–28, **29**, 30
  and cockpit 40–42
  and first manned combat 46–48, 50–51
  and missiles 30–31, 36–40
  and North Vietnam 16–19
  and rockets 31–33, 36
  and shortages 72–73
  and tactical formations **49**
  and training 22–26
Military District No. 4: 76–78
Minh, Nguyen Van 33, **34–35**, 77
Moorberg, Capt M. L. 53
Murray, 1Lt J. E. 57

Na San 19
Nefyedov, Vladimir 13
Ngan, Pham Thanh **16**, 18, 25, 54
  and diversionary sorties 73, **74–75**
  and exhaustion 62, 64–65
  and Phu Ly 33, **34–35**
Nghi, Le Thanh 19
Nghia, Nguyen Van 24, 30–31
Ngu, Dang Ngoc 28, 40, 54, 57, **64**, 76–77
Nhi, Nguyen Hong 17, 25, 38, 43, 46–47, 68–69
Nhu, Bui Duc 18–19, 52, 54, 69, 72
  and Bolo 56–57
Noi Bai 4, 16–17, 19–21
  and targeting 52–53
North Korea 9, 16
North Korean People's Air Force (NKPAF) 59–61
North Vietnam 9, 11, 16–19

Olds, Col R. 56–58, 61
operations:
  Bolo (1967) 56–59
  Rolling Thunder (1965–68) 9, 11

Patterson, Capt R. E. 18
Phu Ly (Ha Nam Province) 33, **34–35**
Phu Tho Province 65, **66–67**, 69, **70–71**
Phuc, Luong The 26

Rabeni, 1Lt J. J. 52
radar 37–38, 51
Radecker, Capt W. S. 57
Rang, Vu Dinh 42
Raspberry, Capt E. T. 57
Reindl, László **25**
Roberts, 1Lt W. E. 62
rockets 31–33, 36
Route Packages 11

Sharp, Adm U. S., Jr. 11
Siu, Tran Ngoc 32, 54
Smith, 1Lt W. T. 46
"Snake" maneuver **45**
Sokolovskiy, Gennadiy 37
Song, Dong Van 42, 46–47, 52
South Vietnam 9
Soviet Union 9, 11, 14–15
  and aircraft supplies 18
  and missiles 36–37
  and pilots 16–17, 59, 72
  and training 22–26
Stone, Capt J. B. 57

US Air Force (USAF) 4–9, 11, 20–21, 64, 73
US Navy 9, 11, 50–51, 76–78

Vietnam People's Air Force (VPAF) 4–8, 11, 16, 19–21
  and pilot exhaustion 61–65, 68–69
  and training 22–26
Vinh 19

weaponry, North Vietnamese 9, 14–15, 27–33, 36–40
Western, 1Lt R. W. 57
Wiggins, 1Lt W. L. 73, **74–75**

Yankee Station, USS 50, 76
Yen Bai 19–21